KT-483-982

david's diary

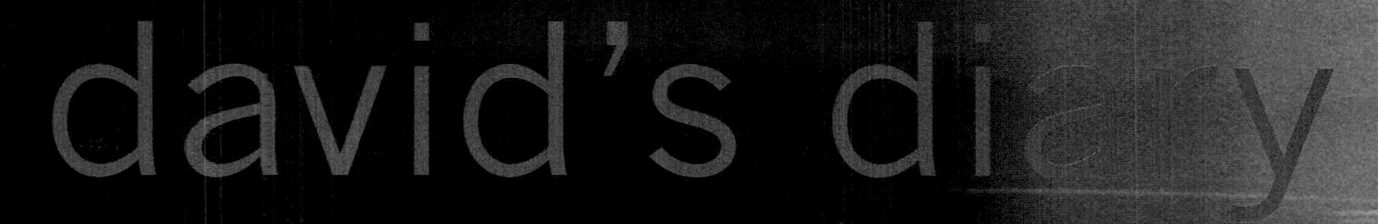

The Quest for the Formula 1 1998 Grand Prix Championship

David Coulthard

with Gerald Donaldson

SIMON & SCHUSTER
A VIACOM COMPANY

For Mum and Dad

First published in Great Britain by Simon & Schuster UK Ltd, 1998
A Viacom company

10 9 8 7 6 5 4 3 2 1

Simon & Schuster UK Ltd
Africa House · 64-78 Kingsway · London WC2B 6AH

Simon & Schuster Australia · Sydney

ISBN 0-684-86179-2

A CIP catalogue record for this book is available
from the British Library

Colour reproduction by DOT Gradations
Printed and bound in Great Britain by Bath Press, Bath

Designed by Peter Ward

contents

West
BOSS
HUGO BOSS
sparco

introduction

Formula 1 is a tremendous sport. I love the pure pleasure, the sensation of driving the most sophisticated racing cars in the world. I love the competition, the wheel-to-wheel battles, with the best drivers. I don't think there is any other sport that gives you the same rewards. I have an interest in football and golf, especially when Scotland is involved, but I cannot imagine anything being a substitute for racing.

I have enjoyed considerable success in my chosen sport, but I've never been a dreamer – in racing, or in life. I have always believed in setting realistic targets and working towards them. If you start with really high expectations you set yourself up for big disappointments, especially in my profession. There is an old saying that in racing the highs are higher and the lows are lower than in any other sport. I try to avoid the peaks and valleys and keep everything on an even keel.

So I was conservative when people asked me what my goal was for the 1998 season. I said my hope was to be running at the front and to win races. I would be happy if I won at least three, which was one more than in 1997. At this stage I was thinking about the minimum it would require to make me satisfied with what I achieved during the season. There is no rocket science involved in this business. Racing is the combination of a car, a driver and a team. If it all gels, and you do your job, the results will be there. Becoming the champion is just an extra bonus for being in front of other competitors more often than not.

> There is no rocket science involved in this business. Racing is the combination of a car, a driver and a team

The media had higher expectations for me, because all the ingredients seemed to be there, for both the McLaren team and myself. Besides the two wins the previous year I should have won at least two other races. I was leading the Canadian Grand Prix when a mechanical problem put me out one lap before the race was over. In the European Grand Prix, the last race of 1997, I was asked by the team to let my team mate Mika Hakkinen past so he could win his first F1 race. As it turned out, after Michael Schumacher lost his points for the season, I was third in the championship, behind the Williams drivers Jacques Villeneuve and Heinz-Harald Frentzen.

West McLaren Mercedes
West
Mobil 1
BOSS
COMPUTER ASSOCIATES
WARSTEINER
Hakkinen
West
8
Mobil 1
BRITISH AEROSPACE
BRITISH AEROSPACE

© Sutton

Our team finished the 1997 season strongly and the theory was that the momentum should still be with us. Granted, we were quietly confident and the new car looked good. But I well remembered 1995, when I was at Williams and we had the best car yet the championship went to Michael Schumacher, then driving for Benetton. That season I also finished third in the standings, behind my team-mate Damon Hill, and I knew how difficult chasing the championship could be, despite having the opportunity to win it. Too many things can go wrong.

Left: Mika and I were starting our third season as team-mates with West McLaren Mercedes. With exactly the same car your team-mate can also be your greatest rival

© Mobil

My reservations about the coming season didn't prevent the media from making me a favourite to become the 1998 World Champion. I read what was said, but it didn't really add to the pressure. There is always pressure to perform. But I want to perform, and one of my harshest critics is named David Coulthard. When I was at Williams in 1995 a lot of people felt happy when I finished second four times in what was my first full Formula 1 season. But I couldn't feel really good about that sort of result because I knew I had not performed at my best. The critic in me was only satisfied when I won my first race, the 1995 Portugese Grand Prix.

Our MP4/13 certainly looked good. But I have never been able to look at a new car and predict that it could be a winner until I have driven it

By the end of February, when our test times were quicker than the others', it became obvious that we had a good car

The first time I saw our 1998 car, officially called the West McLaren Mercedes MP4/13, was at the sneak preview for the press at the McLaren factory in Woking. This was in early February, about a month before the first race. McLaren has always had well-engineered cars, the manufacturing process is first rate, and this new one certainly looked good. But I have never been able to look at a new car and predict that it could be a winner without having driven it. The thing that impressed me most about the MP4/13 was not the big picture. It was the small details.

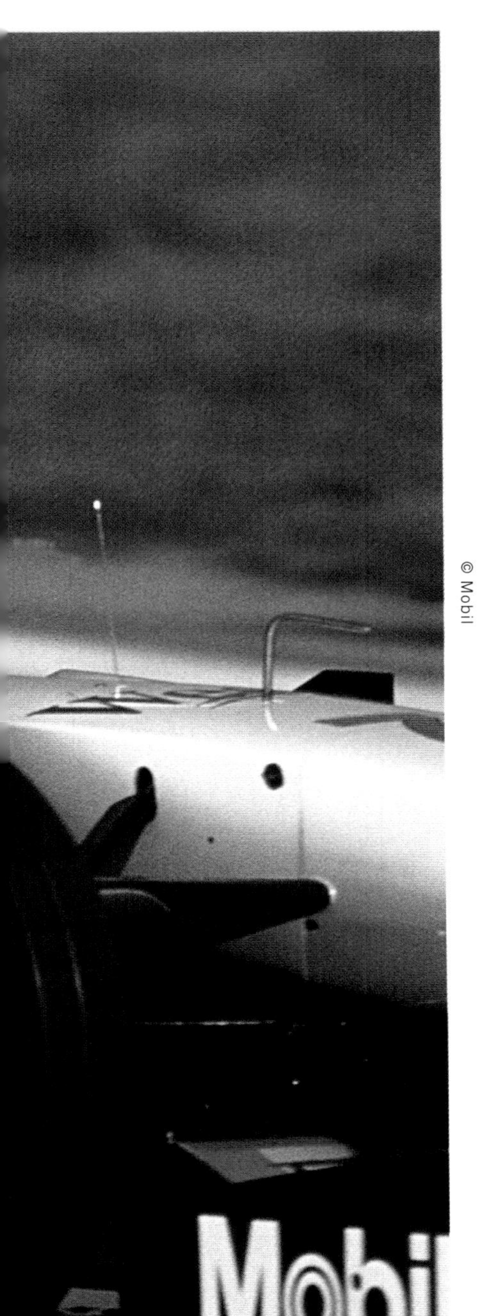

© Mobil

I had no doubt Adrian Newey would make an important contribution to the 1998 car

Adrian Newey took me around the car, pointing out some of the new tweaks and explaining their functions. I had worked with Adrian at Williams and when he came to McLaren as technical director near the end of 1997 I had no doubt he would make an important contribution to the 1998 car.

© Hoch Zwei

But I didn't suddenly start claiming our MP4/13 would be a winner, because with the new design regulations everyone had to start with a clean sheet of paper and there was the possibility another team would come up with a better solution. I was also apprehensive about whether the move to grooved tyres on a narrower chassis would suit my driving style.

Even with the equipment capable of doing the job I knew from past experience how difficult chasing the championship could be

I was nervous that the car would be nervous. I had tested the grooved tyres on the 1997 car with no problems, but having them on the narrower car might make the handling more twitchy than I prefer. It's a weakness and an area I try to work on, but I don't like a nervous car. So there were some doubts. No matter how confident you are as a driver, you have occasional doubts.

When I first took to the track in the MP4/13, at a test in Barcelona, I saw the lap times relative to the others and immediately felt myself growing in confidence. I became relaxed and thought: 'OK, I can do it.' By the end of February, when our times were much quicker than the other teams at the test, it was obvious that we had a good car.

Others had expected it, but up to this point I had treated the predictions about our car a bit like all the rumours you hear in Formula 1. Until I actually experience something first-hand, see it with my own eyes or hear it with my own ears, I tend not to really believe it. I need proof, and we still had to prove ourselves in race conditions.

© Hoch Zwei

© Hoch Zwei/Kunkel

Any reservations I might have didn't prevent the media from making me one of the favourites to become the 1998 World Champion

Compared to most of the other teams we had a late start. Our car was one of the last to appear and we had also made a last-minute switch from Goodyear tyres to Bridgestones, which were still an unknown quantity for us. There hadn't been time to do a full race test with the new equipment and, in terms of preparation, I think we were actually behind where we had been before the first race in 1997. I happened to win that one, in Australia, but I certainly wasn't prepared to say history would repeat itself.

As a friend of mine, David Cawthorne (who grew up with me in the Scottish village of Twynholm), famously says: 'Racing drivers have balls, but not crystal ones.'

Right: **My confidence grew**

© Mobil

Above: **Our technical director Adrian Newey and his first-rate design team had come up with what seemed like a race winner**

© Hoch Zwei

Right: **I happened to win the first race in 1997. Though I wasn't prepared to say history would repeat itself, we were looking good for Australia**

BOSS
West
West
Schweppes

the australian grand prix

melbourne, 8 march

West
7

Melbourne is an enjoyable place to start the season. It's a friendly town and the Albert Park Circuit is in a nice setting. It's fun to drive, though with no high-speed corners it's not particularly challenging. The only nerve-racking thing about it is that it is so far away from base, should you have any problems with the car. We didn't have any big problems, apart from the race result which would cause so much controversy.

Friday 6 March

Intermittent rain meant the first practice session of the new season was mostly inconclusive when it came to determining exactly where we stood in comparison to the other teams, though it seemed we were at least on the pace. In the first hour Mika and I managed to set the quickest times right near the end, when the track began to dry out after a brief shower. Because of the damp conditions we only completed a handful of laps, but there were no technical problems and we concentrated on bedding in our new equipment.

After the first practice session of the new season, it seemed we were at least on the pace

In the final hour of practice Mika was second, behind Michael Schumacher's Ferrari, and I was fifth fastest. My runs were trouble-free but with the track conditions varying from wet to dry the session was not as useful as I would have liked. The few dry runs we had suggested there were some balance and driveability issues which needed to be looked at on my car. The new regulations made the cars more difficult to drive aggressively, especially when you tried to lean hard on them through the corners, and to learn more about that, to understand the behaviour of the car, I needed more running time on a dry track.

With Ron Dennis, the team principal, we decided to adopt a strategy that would put the team's concerns ahead of the drivers' ambitions

Behind the scenes there was also another issue that had to be dealt with – one that

I prefer to 'hit the ground running' on Friday, to get the feel of the track right away and set the tone for the weekend. Not having a proper run meant I didn't get up to speed with the track. At the end of the first day I felt the slow start had put me a bit behind. I had the uncomfortable feeling I would be playing catch-up tomorrow, mentally as well as physically.

Behind the scenes there was also another issue that had to be dealt with – one that would shape the weekend for the team. Before Mika and I drove on Friday a piece of paper was generated for both of us to look at. I chose not to look at mine until Saturday night, after qualifying, though I knew what the document concerned.

To begin the season, because we hadn't done much testing with the new equipment, we were unsure about the reliability of the cars over a race distance. In Melbourne, before we started practice, Mika and I sat down with Ron Dennis, the team principal, Dave Ryan, the team manager, and Adrian Newey. We had a general discussion concerning the best approach for the first two races of the season. It was decided that if we were fortunate enough to be in a position to be in front of the field we would adopt a strategy that would ensure the best result for the team, without putting the cars at unnecessary risk.

It was important that the strategy should be decided as soon as possible, so that neither driver would think the team was trying to favour one over the other. McLaren always stresses a policy of providing equal machinery for its drivers, but to me it's also vital to feel that I'm getting equal treatment on every level, including emotionally. Since Mika has been with the team three years longer than me (he started in 1993) I had sometimes wondered if there might be a natural tendency to show him more favouritism. It is only human nature that this should be the case, and I had talked about it to people on the team. I had always been assured that we had a level playing field, but there were still some nagging doubts. So, it may have been partly for my benefit, to ease my fears, that the rules of engagement in Australia were determined before we went out on the track.

© Hoch Zwei/TAP

The team player still had some nagging doubts

would shape the weekend for the team

I had a fair idea that the drivers would be requested to put the team's concerns ahead of their own ambitions, though I didn't want to know the details just yet, in case dwelling on the implications of that document would interfere with a more immediately important piece of paper: the qualifying timesheet.

© Sutton

As it turned out, the battle for pole position was a private one between Mika and I

Saturday 7 March

In the morning my practice time was quickest, over half a second ahead of Jacques Villeneuve's Williams, but I was not feeling on top of things as much as that advantage might suggest. In fact, I was suprised to be quickest because it took me quite a while to get through my set-up programme and at the end of the session I was still not really comfortable with the car. Not being completely happy about the balance undermined the absolute confidence you need to do your best in qualifying.

As it turned out, the battle for front-row grid positions was a private one between Mika and me. We traded pole position a couple of times, but in the end Mika got it by a fraction of a second. On two of my runs I lost time because I had a touch too much understeer, though right to the end of the qualifying hour I was convinced I could pip him for pole. It all came down to who was able to get a slightly cleaner lap, and Mika managed to do that.

From our superiority in qualifying it was obvious that our cars were the ones to beat, this weekend, at least, but that didn't make our job any easier. It was a bit like when I was at

© Hoch Zwei/Kunkel

Mika and I were requested not to race each other. After the start, whoever got to the first corner first would then remain unchallenged by his team-mate

© Sutton

Williams in 1995. When you've got the best car everyone says it looks easy. But it's not. If the car is faster, it means it's got more grip and downforce, so it's harder to drive. It was bloody hard work from where I was sitting.

Mika and I were nearly a second clear of the third-place car on the grid, Michael Schumacher's Ferrari, so the stage was set for the Australian Grand Prix to be a McLaren race – though, in fact, the outcome of that race would be decided before we arrived at the first corner.

According to the document that had been generated within the team, Mika and I were requested not to race each other. After the start, whoever got to the first corner first would then remain unchallenged by his team-mate, to give us both a better chance of a good finish. We were asked not to race for ourselves, but for the team. As a driver I would have preferred otherwise, but Mika and I both agreed to the strategy. Of course, in my case this put a premium on making a good start, which I have a reputation for being able to do better than a lot of drivers.

Above left: **Win or lose, Heidi would always be there for me**

Above: **With Mika and I setting the fastest times in qualifying, the stage was set for the Australian Grand Prix to be a McLaren race**

From the start Mika led into the first corner. I realised at this moment – all things being equal – that my chances of winning were over

© Mobil

Sunday 8 March

Right: **After leading by about 15 seconds as agreed I let Mika take the win**

© Mobil

In the half-hour warm-up session I worked with my race engineer Pat Fry, trying to get rid of the understeer characteristics that had slightly hampered me so far. We weren't entirely successful and on one lap I made a brief excursion onto the grass. I also lost some time in the pits after a few drops of surplus oil from the engine caused a smoke haze behind the car. My crew cleaned it up and I finished the warm-up with a best time just over a tenth of a second behind the quickest man, my friend Mika.

On the grid we sat for one minute and five seconds waiting for the red lights to go out, which would signal the start of the race. It was a longer delay than usual, because the last car was slow to take up its grid position, and that made a big difference to my start. As we sat there I glanced in my mirrors and saw some smoke coming out of my car's radiators and was worried that the engine might be overheating.

To me, it was obvious. If you make an agreement with someone

It was only a momentary distraction, but enough to interfere with the perfect start I needed to get the jump on Mika into the first corner. It was my fault, because that slight loss of focus meant I only got an average start – which was a real bummer under the circumstances – and Mika led the race.

I made another slight mistake on the opening lap, running wide after the first corner when I glanced in the mirror to see where Michael's red Ferrari was and drifted onto the grass. This momentary bobble gave Michael a chance to take a run at me going into the second corner. Thankfully, his move didn't come off and so the race fell into the agreed strategy, with Mika and me running one-two and opening up a healthy lead over the rest of the field. From then on the race was a walk in the park for McLaren, though my Sunday afternoon in Albert Park was not entirely enjoyable.

Mika and I were so far ahead of the rest that the team kept asking us to go slower and slower, to conserve the cars. We made our first pit stops as scheduled and resumed our front-running positions. Then, to my surprise, with about twenty laps to go Mika suddenly dived into the pits. This was several laps before our second pit stops were due, and I took

– if you look them in the eye and say it – then that's that, as far as I'm concerned

over the lead. I thought Mika must have a problem and now the team would change our pre-determined strategy and the win could be mine after all.

I was still leading Mika by about fifteen seconds after our second pit stops, when I got the bad news. Dave Ryan came on the radio and said Mika's unscheduled stop was a mistake. The team had called him in unnecessarily and he should still be in the lead. I thought about this for a few moments and then got back on the radio. I said, 'OK, I will let him catch me at a second a lap and then let him pass me two or three laps from the end' – because our agreement was still in effect.

To me, it was obvious. If you make an agreement with someone – if you look them in the eye and say it – then that's that, as far as I'm concerned. But since I was making a sacrifice I felt I was entitled to make it quite obvious that I was letting him by. I waited until there were three laps to go and in front of the main grandstand I handed the win back to Mika.

Standing on the second step of the victory podium in Melbourne was not a particularly happy experience. The disappointment of not winning after being in a position to do so was

On the podium with Mika and Heinz-Harald Frentzen, and with mixed feelings about not standing on the top step – where I could have been

not the only thing on my mind. I was having a real problem with having driven so slowly. I knew it was necessary to take it easy on the new car, but as a driver I felt uncomfortable. After fifteen years of trying to make myself go quicker and quicker in racing, getting to a point where it is very difficult to find that last little bit of speed, suddenly here I was in Australia not having to bother with speed.

After the national anthems, the trophy presentations and the champagne-spraying, the confusing thoughts were quickly driven from my mind. When we came down off the podium to face the press all hell broke loose.

I don't think any of us expected the kind of response our 'arranged finish' provoked. The team was accused of fixing the results, depriving the public of its right to entertainment, cheating people who bet on the race out of their money, and so on.

To answer these questions, and some journalists were quite angry, I tried to explain the team's point of view. I mentioned the concerns we had about our reliability. We knew that if Mika and I raced each other there was a chance we would not finish the race. The smart thing to do at this time of year is not to think about entertainment, but to think about scoring points. Sometimes the fastest race is not always the best. Concerning our pre-race agreement, I said I felt obligated to honour it.

I must admit I hadn't considered all the implications, or how people would react to the way we finished the race. In fact, my driver in London, Billy Eldridge, had put a bet on me to win. In Melbourne, my mother and father, who have supported me throughout my career since I was eleven years old, were standing there with three laps to go thinking their son was going to win and, suddenly, they had to deal with him coming second.

In hindsight, maybe we could have handled it better as a team, to make the race result tidier and less controversial. As it was, the team lost respect in some people's eyes, and so did I, for not pushing to the limit the whole way. Racing drivers are supposed to be modern-day gladiators, risking life and limb, and so on. A lot of the public don't understand that sometimes there are team orders and agreements.

At the time we made the agreement we didn't think we were doing anything wrong. But we might have planned for the situation that developed – if one car was leading the race because of a problem with the other car, then the leading car should go on to win. At the next race, providing we were running one-two again, we could have reversed the order, letting the other driver win. In this way the team would get sixteen points from two Grands Prix and everyone would have been happy.

In the post-race interviews Mika stated publicly that he thought what I did was quite

I explained that I felt obligated to honour our pre-race agreement. Mika said he thought what I did was remarkable and thanked me for it

remarkable – very gentlemanly, he said – and he thanked me for it. Ron said it was not a direct team order and that the decision to honour the agreement was mine. He said his drivers should not be criticized for putting the team's considerations ahead of their own, that he was delighted with our sportsmanship and that we hadn't done anything against the spirit of Grand Prix racing. Ron said that after the next race, in Brazil, Mika and I would be free to go hammer and tongs against each other, and that the World Championship would be decided in sixteen races, not one.

Yet I was still feeling uneasy, even guilty, that I had missed the opportunity to take a certain win. As a driver you work so hard to reach the stage where you know how to win, though it is nearly always a difficult thing to do. With our car advantage this would have been the easiest win of my career, but that didn't make it any easier to give it away. Another concern was that a win at the beginning of the season gives you valuable momentum for the next races. Now that momentum was with my team-mate.

With our car advantage this would have been the easiest win of my F1 career. That didn't make it any easier to give it away

© Hoch Zwei

West
West
Mobil

the brazilian grand prix

sao paulo, 29 march

edes-Benz
Bridgestone
West

Reflections

After the Australian race my girlfriend Heidi Wichlinski joined me for a holiday on the island of Bali. Heidi and I have been together for about a year and a half, though our careers keep us apart more often than we would like. With her modelling assignments and my racing we are sometimes on the other side of the world from each other, and with the team's hectic pre-season testing schedule we hadn't seen each other for a while.

I'm not able to give Heidi as much support in her career as she can give me when she comes to the races. She doesn't usually come to the circuit on a Friday because not a great deal is happening then and she would be frustrated hanging around just to see two practice sessions; I would sense her frustration and that would be a distraction. I do feel her support strongly. I don't see her much around the garage but it is comforting to know that she is waiting for me in the motor home out in the paddock.

I don't see her much around the garage but it is comforting to know that Heidi is waiting for me out in the paddock

It's amazing how much she has learned about Grand Prix racing in a short time. She is very good at sussing out people quickly, and forming an opinion about them that is usually spot on. She also has an ability to speak her mind that I don't have. I tend to build up frustrations, and go along with things I don't necessarily agree with, because I am not very good at confrontations. Not that Heidi is confrontational, but she is much better than me at saying what she thinks.

We spent six days at the Bali resort, swimming and taking it easy on the beach. I still felt uneasy about the race result in Melbourne, so I called Jackie Stewart to talk it over with him. Jackie is a good person to ask for advice. I've known him since I was a teenager, and for several seasons I raced with teams he ran with his son Paul. They have their own F1 team now, and besides being a friend and fellow Scot Jackie is very good at seeing the team side of things. He also knows about

I don't necessarily believe that 'nice guys finish last', but then I don't think you can generalize about anything

the public side, because he's been dealing with that kind of thing since he stopped racing in 1973.

I went through the whole scenario with Jackie, and told him about my misgivings over letting Mika win the race. He said he felt I would not come out of it in a bad way, but naturally there might be some doubts in some people's minds about my determination to go for the championship. This bothered me and I wondered if I would have to do something nasty to balance my 'gentlemanly' act in Melbourne.

I don't necessarily believe that 'nice guys finish last', but then I don't think you can generalize about anything. Alain Prost was a nice guy, yet he was aggressive in the car and became the most successful F1 driver of them all. I'm envious of a driver who could win fifty-one Grands Prix, yet do so honourably and not have to barge people out of the way to win. Jackie Stewart was the same kind of driver and won the World Championship three times.

After talking to Jackie I still had some small doubts but felt more comfortable. I appreciate being able to call him up any time and have him willing to take a step back from his busy life to give me a valuable overview. When we got off the phone I was able to put Australia out of my mind and really enjoy the rest of our stay on Bali.

From the bliss of a tropical island the next destination was another island, though rather less exotic and restful. We had a busy test session at Silverstone, followed by a meeting at team headquarters in Woking, with Ron Dennis, Martin Whitmarsh (the team managing director), Adrian Newey, Dave Ryan and Mika.

Everyone had had a couple of weeks to think about what happened in Australia, and we talked the whole thing through. I was assured that the team was not supporting one driver over the other and that there was a firm commitment to balance things out. It was agreed that the team owed me one and that somewhere down the line I would be paid back.

Before the race weekend in Sao Paulo some of us enjoyed a few days' holiday on a private island off the coast of Brazil. The island is owned by a friend of Ron's, who was there with Ron's business partner Mansour Ojjeh. Adrian was with us, too, and the relaxing environment was a good place to solidify our team spirit which, as it turned out, we were going to need more than ever over the next few days.

Following the controversy over our pre-determined one-two finish in Australia, the FIA – the F1 governing body – indicated that in future any obvious attempts to influence race results unduly would be dealt with harshly. There had also been rumours that some of the other teams might protest against what they thought was an illegal braking system on our cars. We didn't expect this to be a problem because the system, operated by an additional brake pedal, had been repeatedly approved by the FIA technical department since we started using it, about halfway through the 1997 season. I didn't think any of this would affect me very much, since it was a technical issue, rather than a driving issue, but it turned out to be a major focus of attention in Brazil.

Globetrotting. Between a holiday in Bali and another on a Brazilian island, we had a test session at Silverstone in England before we went racing in Sao Paulo

Friday 27 March

The Interlagos circuit on the outskirts of Sao Paulo has a strange combination of fast and slow corners which don't really flow together. This makes it difficult to get into a smooth rhythm and because this track, unlike the others, runs in an anti-clockwise direction the g-forces can be hard on your neck muscles. On the positive side Interlagos has been the scene of a lot of F1 history and it gives a younger driver like me a real thrill to drive where heroes like Emerson Fittipaldi once raced. He comes from Sao Paulo and was our team's first World Champion, in 1974, three years after I was born.

In practice we went through our usual programme of balancing the car to the circuit, particularly working on the new tyre construction Bridgestone had brought for this race. While trying to find the limit of grip I slid over a curb, but there was no damage and at the end of the day Mika and I had comfortably set the fastest times. This was satisfying because we were running without the now notorious brake system.

Before we went out on the track several teams protested about our cars, and also those of two other teams that were using similar systems. While the race stewards deliberated the issue we were asked to deactivate the system for the rest of the weekend. We had always contended that our superior pace was the product of the complete package of car and engine – and, of course, the drivers! – and that the brake system was only an incidental advantage. Our practice times proved our point.

Twenty-seven on the 27th. Friday was my birthday and the team's excellent catering staff came up with a cake for a small celebration

© Hoch Zwei

Saturday 28 March

Opposite: **Considering that I never really put together a perfect lap I was happy to end up second on the grid**

Opposite (inset): **On the front row again the McLaren team-mates had a head start for the Brazilian Grand Prix**

While exploring the limits in practice I went over them and had a spin on the Interlagos circuit. All par for the course

My morning practice session was abbreviated somewhat when the car stalled after a spin. I wasn't entirely comfortable with the handling and was losing time to Mika through one particular corner, the third one around the lap. Still, my team-mate and I were again first and second fastest, which turned out to be a forecast of what would happen in the afternoon.

Considering that I never really put together a complete lap in qualifying, I was happy to end up second on the grid. My best time was set on my second run. I cocked up the first and third runs and was prevented from a fourth attempt by a flat battery, caused by a problem with the external cable used to fire up the engine in the pits.

Mika's pole position time was about seven tenths of a second quicker. The third turn, which was still giving me trouble, accounted for a couple of tenths of his advantage, but the fact was he had been quicker all weekend. From the team's point of view both cars were again on the front row, with an even bigger time margin over the opposition than we had had in Australia. This was the best possible response to those who had questioned our brake system, which the stewards, having over-ruled their previous acceptance, had now decided was illegal.

West
Mobil
Computer Associates
Bridgestone

© Hoch Zwei

Formula 1
West McLaren Mercedes
West
DC
Loctite
GRANDE PRÊMIO

Sunday 29 March

My slower start gave Mika an advantage he kept throughout the race

In the warm-up I managed to trim Mika's advantage down to just over a tenth of a second. I was confident about being able to make a race of it, though much would depend on the start. Because we were under such close scrutiny in Brazil we needed to avoid any further questioning of our race results. We discussed the possibility of trying to find a way to help me win, a reversal of what happened in Australia, but the eventuality of such a scenario seemed remote. Mika and I would also still have to be careful not to put finishing at risk on a circuit where it is so difficult to pass, especially in such evenly matched cars. If I was to win, all these considerations made a good start even more important than usual.

I didn't get the start I needed. Drivers always have a book full of excuses and mine was that the starting grid at Interlagos is on a slight incline. It's similar to making a start when your road car is parked on a hill. You have to co-ordinate the brake, clutch and accelerator to get away smoothly. In our racing cars we also have the option of using a hand clutch on the steering wheel. Mika uses it, but I'm not as accustomed to it. One time I used the hand clutch and stalled the engine. That memory made me apprehensive about using it here, though it would be an advantage.

So there I was on the starting grid, arguing with myself over which clutch to use – not the ideal way to begin a race. At the last minute – make that the last second – I decided to use the foot clutch, which meant my right foot was on the brake and throttle at the same time. This decision may have cost me the race. It certainly cost me the start, because Mika was ahead as we went into the first corner, and that's the way we finished.

© Sutton

© Vinet/Sutton

Above: **By pushing him hard . . .**

. . . I kept my team-mate on his toes

© Sutton

© Sutton

Michael Schumacher was third. His first appearance on the podium was a forecast of the Ferrari challenge that was to come

Opposite: The scoreboards. 'P2' and 'P1' meant 6 points for Scotland, 10 for Finland and the maximum for McLaren

A couple of times during the race I closed right up on Mika, but it would have taken some kind of incident – a mistake on his part, or a mechanical problem – for me to get past. I started to lose the grip from my rear tyres a little bit sooner than he did. I thought it might be better to see if I could cool them for a few laps and then maybe his tyres would go off and I would try to push again as we got nearer the pit stops. But when I tried to push again I didn't have any extra grip. There was some extra near the end but not enough to mean I could challenge Mika. Overall, I was mostly a little slower than him. I was having some difficulties with traction out of the last corner and then, near the end of the race, my neck started to give out.

I was having some difficulties with traction out of the last corner and then, near the end of the race, my neck started to give out

It causes me a bit of embarrassment that this should have happened, because I am supposed to be one of the fittest drivers; and I'm certainly much fitter now than I have ever been at any stage in my career. But I don't specifically work on my neck. Most of the strengthening of my neck muscles comes from driving a racing car. Nearly all the driving is done in a clockwise direction, so that after seventy-two laps in the opposite direction around the Interlagos circuit my neck muscles were a little bit tired. It probably didn't affect my lap times much, because in the corners I rested my head on the side of the car, but it added to the discomfort of finishing second.

In truth, it was all I deserved. I felt I had underperformed all weekend, that Mika had the edge. Under the circumstances the six points for second place was acceptable.

America

I enjoy being in America, where F1 racing is not such a high-profile sport and you can wander around unnoticed

Before we headed south for the next race, in Argentina, I flew to north to Florida and spent a week visiting my old friends Gil and Angela de Ferran in Fort Lauderdale. I've known them for many years, since Gil and I raced together earlier in our careers. Gil is in IndyCar racing, where he is a frontrunner, and we had a happy time comparing notes. The de Ferran family now includes Anna, their first child. I am honoured to be Anna's godfather and it was a delight to see her.

I enjoy being in America, where F1 racing is not such a high-profile sport and you can wander around unnoticed. We went to Disneyland for a couple days, and had an enjoyable time communing with Mickey Mouse. But it wasn't all fun and games. We also took advantage of the fitness facilities in America, which are more advanced and widespread than in Britain and Europe. The major hotels all have large gyms full of sophisticated equipment. We stayed in one of them, where my trainer Jerry Powell and I spent many hours working out.

I was always fairly fitness conscious but only really started to focus on it from a racing point of view in 1991, when I was preparing to move from F3 into F3000 cars. The further up you go in racing the more important fitness becomes, and in F1 racing it is vitally important. When Jerry Powell, a highly trained fitness expert, came to McLaren at the end of 1996 he devised a training programme for me that was much more race-specific.

The emphasis is not so much on developing the 'posing' muscles on the biceps and chest, the ones that you see weightlifters flexing mightily. In the car you do need extra upper-body strength to handle the wheel and withstand the tremendous g-forces generated in braking and accelerating, and especially in cornering. But the way you sit in the cockpit, in a reclining position with your knees bent, also places great stress on your knees and the smaller muscles in your hips and lower back. With Jerry I concentrate on strengthening these muscles to prevent them from cramping and fatiguing the way they can over a race distance.

The focus on the lower body also brings into play the old Chinese philosophy that all human power comes from the legs. Someone with strong legs is very difficult to push over, because you control your whole body from the muscles that come through the pelvis into your legs.

Besides the practical consideration of being fit enough to handle the physical demands of driving the car, knowing that you are physically strong can also help you psychologically. As a driver you're always trying to gain an advantage and you can get extra mileage from the inner belief that you are stronger than your rivals. Working very hard on the fitness aspect of racing gives me confidence that I would never have to back off in wheel-to wheel battles for physical reasons.

The competition factor also enters into my relationship with Jerry. He is a good guy, always upbeat, positive-thinking and smiling, and there is a friendship between us. But when we are training together he is also a keen competitor and that helps push me on to the next level of fitness.

Heidi and my trainer Jerry Powell are always upbeat, though Jerry's heavy-duty workouts sometimes wipe the smile off my face

Another advantage of being fit is the stamina it provides. The fitter you are the less time it takes to recover from a race. I feel that I have more than enough in reserve to go a race distance on a Sunday, and then go testing again on the following Monday, which we often have to do.

By the end of the week in Florida, the combination of sweating through hard workouts with Jerry and pleasant socializing with the de Ferrans had put me in the perfect frame of mind to tackle the Argentine Grand Prix.

the
argentine
grand prix
buenos aires, 12 april
Mobil

West
Sun
Sun
COMPUTER
7
7

Friday 10 April

I was reasonably confident of my chances in Argentina, where we expected our car advantage to continue. Of course, this meant that Mika would also be quick. In the race, providing he got to the front, it was likely he would be consistent and not make many mistakes. The ideal situation for me would be to get pole, make a better start, keep out of trouble and win. Such perfection, though very difficult to achieve, is every driver's dream. The first part of my dream came true. Unfortunately, a hard dose of reality made my race a bit of a nightmare.

Buenos Aires is a beautiful city, but the Autodromo on its outskirts is something like a go-kart track for F1 cars. The lap distance of over two and a half miles is crammed into a small amount of land, so that you spend most of the time braking and cornering. The lack of long straights means that you can never really get wound up and overtaking opportunities are few and far between, and that makes it frustrating to race on. That said, I managed to find a useful way around it on my first visit here, in 1995, and I got pole position.

In the first hour of practice, when we had both damp and dry track conditions to contend with, I was second quickest and Mika was third. At the top of the timesheets it was a bit disconcerting to see Michael Schumacher's Ferrari. In the final hour, when the track dried out after a brief shower, I managed to set the fastest time. Michael was still there, in second place, followed by Mika.

A dream result in Argentina would be to get pole position and win. Part of it came true, but my race was a bit of a nightmare

West
KENWOOD
7

Saturday 11 April

In morning practice Michael set the pace. was second quickest, after a spin, and Mika, who at one point ran down an escape road, was fourth. We worked hard all morning to balance the cars in response to the track conditions that were again changing from wet to dry. We were also working hard in response to Michael's surprising performance. If this was an accurate forecast it seemed his Ferrari was set to challenge our supposed supremacy, and qualifying, if not the race, would be very close. And so it was – too close for comfort.

Opposite: **A damp surface made the track tricky in practice. The closeness of the times between the two McLarens and the Ferrari made qualifying tense**

Qualifying was a very tense affair – a shoot-out between the two McLarens and the Ferrari. After our first runs I was second, behind Michael and ahead of Mika. Michael maintained his advantage after the second runs. Only about four hundredths of a second separated us and with twenty minutes to go I had one last chance to get pole.

© Sutton

© Hoch Zwei

As I sat in the car in the garage waiting for an opportune moment to go out, it seemed Mika was no longer part of the equation. He just didn't seem to have got himself into the highest gear on the weekend and I felt pretty comfortable that I had could set a quicker lap time than him. But the

Waiting in the garage with a few minutes remaining I thought about my one last chance to get pole position

I was so happy that if I hadn't been strapped tightly in the car I felt I could have done backflips like a gymnast!

© Sutton

I was so happy about getting pole it felt as if I had won a race instead of just the right to be a few feet further ahead on the starting grid

Michael factor was something I hadn't expected in qualifying, and it was obviously going to require a special effort to beat him.

For a really quick lap there are two areas of the circuit that you have to get absolutely right. One is the first corner, because it is such a long corner, and the other is turn 4, which is also quite long. Because they are so important you can sometimes be too cautious on the approach and apply the mental brakes so that you don't overcook it and fly off the road. But I thought to myself, I must give it absolutely everything I had. I needed to be totally on the limit everywhere to get pole position. When I came through the second of the two long corners and found I was already four tenths of a second quicker than my previous run, all I had to do was keep the rest of the lap neat and tidy and that should do the trick. I crossed the line about half a second quicker and beat Michael to the pole.

I was so happy that if I hadn't been strapped tightly in the car I felt I could have done backflips like a gymnast! It felt so good because winning pole is not something I'd done that often – only five times previously in my F1 career. It was so satisfying, because I put so much effort into it, kept focused, concentrated hard, didn't let the pressure get to me and got the absolute maximum out of the car. In a way it felt as if I'd won a race instead of just the right to be twenty-six feet further ahead on the starting grid.

© Sutton

Sunday 12 April

In the warm-up, when it was overcast and the damp track was drying progressively, I was eighth quickest and quite happy with the way the car handled in race trim. t was heavy, carrying a lot of fuel to accommodate our one-stop strategy. The extra weight would hinder

outright speed in the early part of the race, but if everything went my way it shouldn't be a problem. I was confident that if I got to the first corner first it would be very difficult for anyone to overtake me on this track.

My start was a good one and after two laps I was nearly three seconds ahead of Mika, who was being pressured by Michael. A couple of laps later Michael moved into second place, by which time I was experiencing some difficulty with the gearbox. A slight hesitancy when downshifting meant I was having trouble slowing down for corners. To compensate I was braking earlier than usual, but on the fifth lap I didn't quite slow the car enough on the approach to turn 8, a right-hand hairpin bend.

After my good start, Michael took second from Mika. His method of taking the lead from me I found completely unacceptable

© Glockner/Sutton

I realized that Michael was close behind me, but I did not believe he would make a move that would risk putting us both out of action

I went into the corner a bit crossed up, applying opposite lock, and running wide on the exit. I managed to get it together again, only to feel an almighty thump. The next thing I knew I was in the air and a red car shot beneath me and into the lead.

I had realized Michael was close behind me, but I did not believe he would position himself at a place on the track where we might have a coming-together. Never mind the danger factor, there is just no logic in anyone making such a move that would risk putting themselves, let alone another competitor, out of action.

My immediate reactions were surprise at what had happened, then anger because I thought my race was over, and finally disappointment that I had surely lost a golden opportunity to win. As it developed, I was able to keep the car going, and rejoined the track. The car was looking a bit battle-scarred and I was worried about possible suspension or steering damage. But once I got up to speed everything seemed to be in fairly good working order. I was now in sixth place and since there were still sixty-seven laps to go I went racing again.

I made good progress, and was up as high as fourth before my pit stop about halfway through the race. When I came back out I quickly caught up to Jacques Villeneuve's Williams and sat on its gearbox for several laps, looking for a way by. On lap 52 an opportunity presented itself at the Senna S section of the circuit, where Jacques got really sideways on the exit. I was much quicker than him going into that turn and while he was busy trying to sort out his problem I pulled around him on the outside. He started to turn in towards me, so I

© Glockner/Sutton

went wider but it wasn't far enough. His Williams smashed into the left rear corner of my car and we both spun.

I think Jacques thought he could just barge his way through. If you're going to run into each other you have to be prepared not to finish, and that's what happened to Jacques. In my mind at the time, I felt he deserved it. I managed to keep going, though my car was looking distinctly second-hand. A rear wheel was bent, a sidepod and winglet were damaged, and the floor was broken. But McLaren builds strong cars and now, with a lighter fuel load, I was able to lap as quickly as Michael, who was on his way to winning the race.

The incident with Jacques had put me down into seventh place and I was determined to at least collect a point by climbing back to sixth. That would require overtaking Jean Alesi's Sauber, a manouevre I attempted on lap 66, at the scene of my confrontation with Jacques. Coming into the Senna S my car sailed straight on, losing grip on oil somebody had spilled on the previous lap, and I disappeared down the escape road. Once again, and thankfully for the last time in the race, I was able to get back on track and I finished in sixth place.

My Argentine Grand Prix was a catalogue of cock-ups. After all that went on I suppose I should have been happy just to survive, but I wasn't, really. I was very disappointed. There was a classic opportunity to get ten points, and I came away with only one. It was a bitter pill to swallow, and the incidents with Jacques and Michael bothered me. I talked it over with both of them later.

> I went into the corner a bit crossed up . . . The next thing I knew I was in the air and a red car shot beneath me and into the lead

© Sutton

Making up for lost time I was able to climb back to sixth at the finish and collect a point

Opposite: The collision with my friend Jacques Villeneuve, the reigning World Champion, was easier to take than the incident with Michael

Jacques said our coming together was more his fault than mine, though I would have been prepared for him to say he thought I turned into him a bit early. On reflection, I realized the move I made on him was always going to be risky, because I know it s Jacques' nature not to give an inch in a wheel-to-wheel confrontation. So I felt I had contributed to the incident and told him I regretted saying earlier that he didn't deserve to finish.

I strongly believe in racing etiquette. I think it's wrong to get alongside somebody and squeeze them off, though that was never my intention with Jacques. Sometimes you can give an opponent a little nudge to make them realize you are there, but it is bloody stupid and dangerous to deliberately run into someone and drive them off the track. That's not sport and that's why I had trouble with Michael's move on me.

I felt I was cautious about what I said about it publicly because, apart from anything else, I had had an hour and a half in the car to think about it before I talked to anyone. I always

GOODYEAR
Castrol
SONAX
Castrol
SONAX
VELTINS
VELTINS
FUJITSU
FALKE
FALKE
FALKE
VELTINS
CHAMPION
West
DC

Opposite: **The bottom line was that my driving had been good enough to win races and that was something I needed to do as quickly as possible**

It was Michael's opinion, he said, that I closed the door on him, which I totally disagree with

maintain that if anyone can keep their anger for that long they are either a very angry person or they are putting on an act about how they are feeling at the time.

I admit that I contributed to the first part of the incident, by making a mistake and running wide, thus giving Michael the opportunity to have a go at me. The second part, him running into me, I think was totally unacceptable. He had a clear view of what was going on and must have known what the consequences might be. He said he had the line into the corner, was committed to it and had the momentum, so why should he back off?

That made me really angry, because he actually accelerated into me. You could see it on the video of the incident. We watched it together, when we flew out of Argentina on the same plane. It was Michael's opinion, he said, that I closed the door on him, which I totally disagree with. I think it is the responsibility of the guy behind – in this case Michael (and in several other incidents during his career) – to avoid contact with the guy in front. If you ran into the side of someone like this a few years ago in F1, someone would have been killed. The cars and circuits are much safer now and, unfortunately, it seems the sport has changed to the point where it has become almost acceptable to barge into people.

On that flight home on Sunday night I thought about where I stood after the first three races. After finishing second to Michael in Argentina Mika had 27 points, Michael had 14 and I had an unlucky 13. My father talks a lot about the championship but I prefer to judge my performance by looking at each race individually.

In Australia I had performed well enough to win, though the team agreement left me second. In Brazil second was all I deserved. In Argentina a possible win was also denied by circumstances that were largely out of my control. The bottom line was that, though there was certainly room for improvement, my driving had been good enough to win races and that was something I needed to do as quickly as possible.

© Hoch Zwei

the san marino grand prix

imola, 26 april

RTL
sparco

The Media

Some people say you shouldn't read what is written about you. But I am a fan of the sport. I love motor sport and have done so my whole life. I want to know all about it in its many forms. The only way to keep in touch with what's happening, especially when you're a very busy racing driver, is to read all about it. When I read the papers and magazines after we got back to Europe there were many comments about my race performances to date.

As I expected, there were two different points of view about the incident with Michael in Argentina. On one side there were those who praised the brilliance of Michael and the way he muscled his way past me to win. It was speculated that I was a 'shrinking violet' and lacked aggression. On the other side of the coin were those journalists who wrote that Michael was, once again, overly aggressive and had pushed yet another victim out of the way.

I still felt that I couldn't have done anything more than I did to stop Michael from passing me, by simply holding my line. If you are doing that and another car hits you, and sends you spinning up into the air, there should be no question about the guy in the airborne car lacking aggression. Anyone saying that really doesn't understand what it is like in a racing car.

Then there were comments concerning my letting Mika win in Australia. The point of view that I had acted honourably according to our agreement was offset by some, who felt that after what happened in Australia and Argentina it seemed that I was 'too gentlemanly' and not nasty enough to be a champion. One journalist even wrote that he would have more respect for me if I had got out of the car in Buenos Aires, grabbed Michael by the throat and punched him in the face.

As a fan of the sport I love reading about it. But being a focus of so much media attention is a mixed blessing

Opposite: **There was no need to raise my aggression level. In the past some thought it was too high and I was called a complete nutter**

The fact is I am racing here and now, and my approach to the sport has served me well

I find this attitude completely laughable. I think it is farcical that nowadays in sport things have deteriorated to the point that you have to commit violence against an opponent to get any respect. If my attitude means that I would be better suited to bygone eras when what mattered most was that you played the game fairly, then so be it. The fact is I am racing here and now, and my approach to the sport has served me well. I can battle as hard as the best of them. I don't think any of my peers would say I'm a soft touch in a race. In fact, in 1995 my aggression prompted Jean Alesi – who has a reputation for being one of the more aggressive drivers – to say I was a complete nutter.

The written word also contained gossip about Michael Schumacher replacing me next season at McLaren. No matter how hard you try to ignore this kind of thing it is aggravating and can also be unsettling if you start to believe it. And, of course, when something is written in one paper the others ask you to respond. I said that at my best I can perform as well as Michael, though he has been more consistent with his results, and I pointed out that I had managed to beat him several times.

I know that much of what is written in the press is intended to sell newspapers and magazines. All I ask is that what is written about me is balanced and fair. If I feel it isn't I don't hesitate to seek out the author and talk it over privately. It's the same if I have a problem with a driver. I try to avoid speaking to them or sending a message to them through the press. I prefer to talk to them personally, sit down with them man to man and discuss it in a mature way.

Thursday 23 April

At Imola, the day before practice began, I had the opportunity to present some of my views publicly at a press conference at the circuit. I was slightly agitated when I arrived because Heidi and I had chosen to drive from Monaco and heavy traffic meant a longer journey than expected. I am not a fan of long car trips and after about four and a half hours fighting traffic on congested Italian autostradas I was in a good mood to deal with inquisitive journalists.

Interestingly, Michael and Jacques had also been selected to appear before the media in the press conference. One of the first questions I was asked was how to define a 'racing incident', the term being used to describe the collisions with Michael and Jacques, where it was judged none of us was to blame.

I said that there isn't a book which defines the correct procedure for overtaking in an F1 race, but maybe there should be. Much of the time it comes down to the two drivers involved, because only they know the lines they should be on. If you have enough time to know where you are on the track, and what you are doing at that moment, you will know

West

My goal for this race was to turn my season around – by driving well, getting in front and staying there

whether what you have done is normal and fair, or incorrect and unfair. But ultimately it is the race stewards who will make the judgement on these matters. Sometimes they pick up incidents which hardly merit discussion and impose penalties on whoever is decided to be the guilty party. Other times they turn a blind eye to major incidents which clearly deserved to be punished.

I said I was surprised that the three of us involved in the incidents in Argentina were not called up before the stewards and questioned about our actions. By speaking about it publicly I hoped it might stimulate some debate that could lead to developing a code of acceptable conduct for drivers. In one way, this is my responsibility, since I am a representative of the Grand Prix Drivers Association. The other two GPDA representatives, nominated by the rest to present the drivers' point of view to the F1 authorities, are Damon Hill and Michael Schumacher.

My position was that we need to know what rules we are playing by. In boxing low blows are treated as fouls, but in racing it seems there are many interpretations of what constitutes a low blow and the referees don't decide which interpretation to use until long after a blow has been levelled. Granted, racing is more difficult to police than boxing, but kidney punching should be illegal in any sport.

Anyway, at Imola someone wanted to know if I would now step up my aggression level. I said that I hadn't had a problem with my ability to race aggressively in the past. If you were to look at the factors that make a racing driver, I don't think that my ability to race hard is one that should be questioned. Sometimes you come off best in incidents and sometimes you don't. The only reason I was being asked this question was because I came off worse in the last Grand Prix. But one race is not what you base your opinion of a driver's career on.

I'm very comfortable with the way I race within what I believe are reasonable rules of behaviour. I believe you have to respect the other driver and the piece of track that he is on. Some drivers make a point, either through their talk or their actions, of developing a reputation for being ruthless and unwilling to give way, come hell or high water. I'm not afraid to show to my competitors, to let them know right up front, that I would never deliberately drive someone off the track or put them into a wall. That doesn't mean that I won't squeeze them as far as I think is safe. That is a fundamental in racing. But you have to have respect and trust the people around you.

© Sutton

Heidi and I share a not very private moment before the start of a weekend that would be memorable

In answer to a question about whether I was going to change my approach in any way, I said that my main goal was simply to make sure that I got in front and stayed there. In that way I hoped to turn my season around. I was third in the championship at the moment, with thirteen races to go, so I would just have to get stuck in and try to get the results I was looking for.

I believe you have to respect the other driver and the piece of track that he is on

But I also said I'm always looking at areas I can improve, whether it is with my driving or the way I work with the car and the engineers. That is a constant battle. You don't achieve a certain level as a F1 driver and just stay there. You always have to keep pushing yourself harder and pushing the limits. That is part of what I enjoy about racing.

The last question I was asked at Imola was whether I would want to take Michael around for a few laps in the new McLaren two-seater car. The car, a near replica of our racing cars except for the passenger seat behind the driver, would soon be ready for its first run. I said giving Michael a ride would be great publicity for West McLaren Mercedes but probably not so good for Ferrari. I wouldn't want to be driven in that car by anyone, though it would be fun to see the faces of a passenger once they get out of it, because I really think the experience would be a very big shock. I suggested that the person in the press room who was thought to have the biggest head, or the biggest ego or the biggest mouth, should be singled out by all the journalists and put in the back of the car. I was sure it would be a humbling experience for them and they would probably be very sick after one lap.

Friday 24 April

I quite like Imola. It's called the Autodromo Enzo e Dino Ferrari because the Ferrari factory is near by and the track has a lot of history, some good and some very sad. It was here in 1994 that Roland Ratzenberger and Ayrton Senna were killed in one of the sport's worst weekends. Following those tragedies the track was modified for safety reasons, but it still offers interesting challenges. The layout is like a smaller version of Monza, Italy's other circuit, though with shorter straights and lower speeds. I had normally driven well here and my confidence level was still high after being so quick in qualifying in Argentina.

I like Imola and getting into the groove quickly in practice gave me confidence to really go for it in qualifying

© Hoch Zwei

I carried that confidence onto the track and it grew even higher when I got into a groove straightaway in practice. If you have a bad start on Friday, if you don't get the car working properly, it is very difficult to catch that up come Saturday and qualifying. Mika ended up being slightly quicker, but I knew that wasn't necessarily an accurate reflection of where I stood in comparison. A small engine problem meant I couldn't finish the end of the session and missed out on the chance to check the car on new tyres. Tomorrow was another day, and one that I felt very optimistic about.

Saturday 25 April

By throwing everything I had into my best lap I reacted positively to the pressure and got my second pole position in succession

In morning practice I was quickest, by eight tenths of a second over Mika, even though I spent much of the session working with different set-ups to try to reduce the understeer I had been experiencing while turning into the corners.

After the first qualifying runs I was fastest. Then, when we changed the set-up to reduce the understeer so I could attack the corners harder, Mika nipped ahead. For my third run we returned my car to its original settings. Three quarters of the way through the lap I was a couple of tenths slower than Mika's time, so I threw everything I had into the final sector and finished up on pole by a tenth of a second over Mika.

It was my second pole in succession and very satisfying to get it. There was an element of relief to it because I had made it hard work for myself. Near the end, I knew Mika had improved, and that it was always going to be tight. So it was a good feeling to go out and do what I had to do, and react positively to the pressure of qualifying.

Sunday 26 April

In the warm-up I was fastest by a considerable margin and felt very content with the car in race trim. The spare car was set up for me this weekend and I even had time to check it out for a few laps. Mika wound up fourth quickest after losing time with boiling brake fluid. I had a similar problem but chose not to come in and have the brakes bled the way he did.

To me, this was an indication that Mika was not as settled in his mind as I was. In a situation like this both drivers are thankful, in a way, that they are suffering with the same problem. It's easier to deal with in your mind when you know fate hasn't singled you out. But it seemed like a

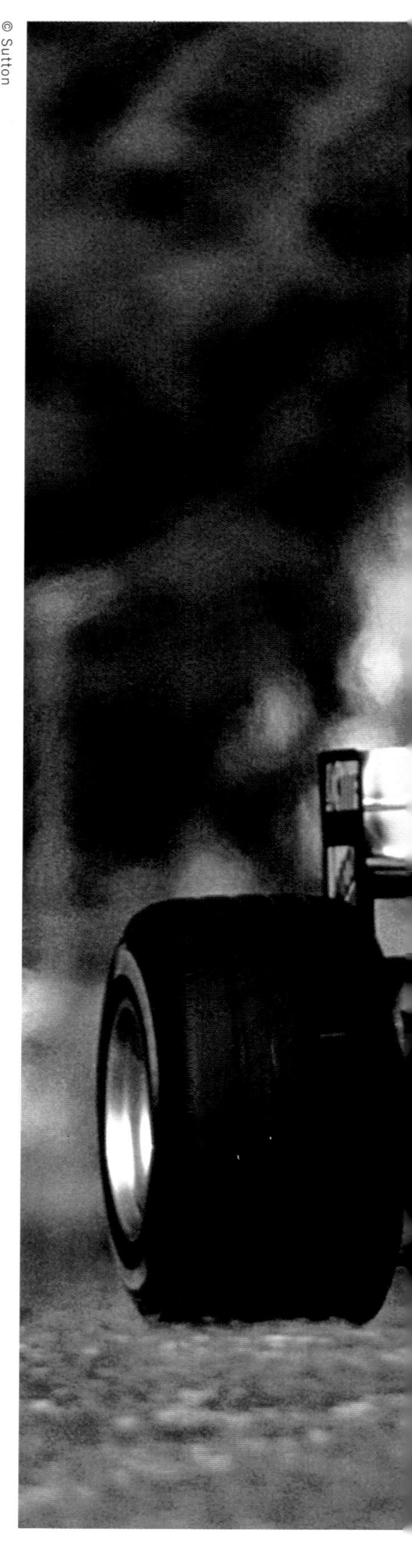

© Sutton

© Sutton

negative attitude to come in and have the brakes bled. They were not going to fail in a half-hour warm-up session and Mika missed an opportunity to do a better time. My attitude was to go ahead and do another run and worry about it afterwards. I felt Mika's uncertainty showed a lack of confidence, and that gave me even more momentum.

Before the race the drivers were taken around the track on the customary tour to show the fans our faces without our helmets on. This being Ferrari's home circuit the tifosi, as the

WARS

At the start I got away smoothly, concentrated on building up a gap to Mika and Michael, and eased away into a lead I never lost

fanatical Ferrari fans are called, were there in their tens of thousands. At one corner, amongst a sea of Ferrari flags and banners, a lone Scottish flag was being waved. I joked that it was embarrassing because I told my Mum not to go in there with the tifosi. My feeble attempt at humour was actually reported in a prominent paper.

At the start I got away smoothly and concentrated on building up a gap to Mika, in case there was a problem in my pit stop. I felt very comfortable in front but was careful not to

© Sutton

© Sutton

Mika later dropped out with a mechanical problem, but my car never skipped a beat, much to the disappointment of the fanatical Ferrari fans

push too hard. There was no need to be on the limit at every corner, and as I had not won a race yet it would be foolish to risk making a mistake. I just quietly eased away.

The early laps went by without incident and then on lap 17 I was informed over the radio that Mika was out of the race. I didn't see his car anywhere on the circuit so I presumed he had retired in the pits, which meant it was unlikely he had an engine failure. A few laps later I was instructed to short shift – shift gears earlier than usual at a lower rpm.

I never questioned why the team wanted me to do this, though I suspected it had something to do with whatever Mika's problem had been. I didn't want to have to worry about it. When your team mate has a mechanical failure you have to be prepared for a similar problem in your car, but there is very little you can do about it other than follow the team's instructions. You don't want any unneccesary information. As it turned out Mika had a gearbox problem, but there seemed to be nothing wrong with mine.

Everything continued to go fairly smoothly and on lap 44 I peeled off into the pits to make my second stop. I came in

Shell
Shell

WARSTEINER · BEER · WARSTEINER · BEER · WARSTEINER · BEER · WARSTEINER

slowly to avoid overheating the brakes and the guys put in the fuel and changed the tyres with their usual efficiency. When I regained the circuit I immediately saw in my mirrors a red Ferrari. I then wondered at the wisdom of being so cautious on the entry to the pits, because I wasn't sure if the Ferrari behind me was being driven by Michael or Eddie Irvine, who had been running second and third.

Since I was quite busy trying to get the most out of my new tyres I didn't want to ask over the radio which Ferrari was behind me. When you're concentrating hard a conversation can be distracting and any information you receive may not be immediately absorbed. So I focused on keeping the gap to the Ferrari and when I came around after the first lap my lead had actually increased. At this point I became more relaxed because if I could open up the gap with a full load of fuel and new tyres I was obviously in good shape.

It is an amazing rush of emotion that flows through your whole body when you win

It was Michael in the following Ferrari. He made a pit stop, after which he began to close up on me quite quickly. To counteract this threat Dave Ryan came on the radio and said I should go back to normal shifting. It was funny, because Dave said I needed to do a certain lap time to maintain the gap to Michael, and when I came around again I had actually gone a tenth of a second quicker than instructed. I felt like going on the radio and apologizing.

It was important to let Michael know that he could chase me all he wanted but if he got too close I could still go quicker than him. If you are chasing someone and they start to open up a bigger gap it can be demoralizing and they tend to back off. That's what Michael did and he settled for second place.

On the final lap I spoke to the team over the radio, saying my usual thing when I am about to win: 'Here I come!' All the guys were leaning over the pit wall as I crossed the

All the guys were leaning over the pit wall as I came over the finish line. I jinked over and gave them a bit of a victory wiggle

One happy Scottish F1 driver

finish line and I jinked over close and gave them a bit of a victory wiggle.

It is an amazing rush of emotion that flows through your whole body when you win. I certainly don't get that feeling in anything else I do in life. It's an overwhelming feeling of joy, a physical sensation that is almost sexual.

This victory was especially satisfying because it was so timely. I had to come here and do exactly what I did. It is important not to allow people a comfort zone. That gives them extra confidence, so I had to take pole and lead from the start. When you're under such pressure you have to take yourself back to the core of your self-belief and motivation. You have to keep reminding yourself that you have what it takes to do the job. When you get proof of that, with a win, it can put you on a roll.

In the post-race interviews I made a point of saying that my result was the best response to the earlier criticism, and to the rumours that my future in the team was not secure. It brought me to within three points of Mika in the championship, which meant the team would continue to focus on us both. If Michael had retired, it would have been perfect, but I was still three points ahead of him.

There was no partying or celebrating after the race because I was actually feeling unwell. I had a very sore stomach, probably from something I ate, and had to lie down for a couple of hours in the back of the team motor home. Heidi and I didn't leave the circuit until late and it was well after midnight when we got home to Monaco. The next day I was involved in a Mercedes 'A' Class promotion with Mika and Ron near Nice, and that night we went to Barcelona to begin a week's testing.

The fourth win of my F1 career was especially satisfying because it was so timely

West
West
Mercedes-Benz
Mercedes-Benz
West
BOSS
West

the spanish grand prix

barcelona, 10 may

10
WORLD CHAMPIONSHIP

Teamwork

Barcelona was only two weeks later, though Imola already seemed a very long time ago by the time we came to race in Spain. I made my F1 debut in the 1994 Spanish Grand Prix, but have few feelings of nostalgia for either the place or that occasion. I don't very often look back on the past and tend to live my life for today.

Before I went to Barcelona I was cleaning out filing cabinets and sorting through piles of documents in boxes that hadn't been unpacked since I moved to my flat in Monaco three years ago. I threw out a lot of old Grand Prix stuff, thinking it was no good to me now.

I prefer to be as organized as possible and with the business side of my career becoming increasingly complicated I recently set up a company, David Coulthard Associates. Our office is in England and run by my old friend Iain Cunningham. I've known Iain since I was a wee lad and being a fellow Scot he understands both me and the language. He also understands the commercial and marketing side of racing because he worked with Frank Williams for a long time, and also spent some time at Paul Stewart Racing in the years I raced there. Iain is someone I can trust and so is Martin Brundle, the retired F1 driver who now works with Murray Walker as a commentator on the ITV television coverage of the races. Martin is available to advise me on driver-related matters and his wide experience in dealing with the often complex issues that a driver faces outside racing is also useful.

Though you're alone in the car on the track F1 racing is still very much a team effort. Including the personnel back at the factory, West McLaren Mercedes has over three hundred people. It's impossible to get to know everyone but naturally you become closer to the people who go to the races. There are about sixty people on our race team, nine of them working directly on my car.

With 158 Grands Prix to his credit Martin Brundle is well-equipped to advise me on driver-related matters, both on and off the the track

West
Mobil 1
Mercedes-Benz
BOSS
POTENZA
BRIDGESTONE
COMPUTER ASSOCIATES
7

It is important to me to have a good relationship with everyone on the team

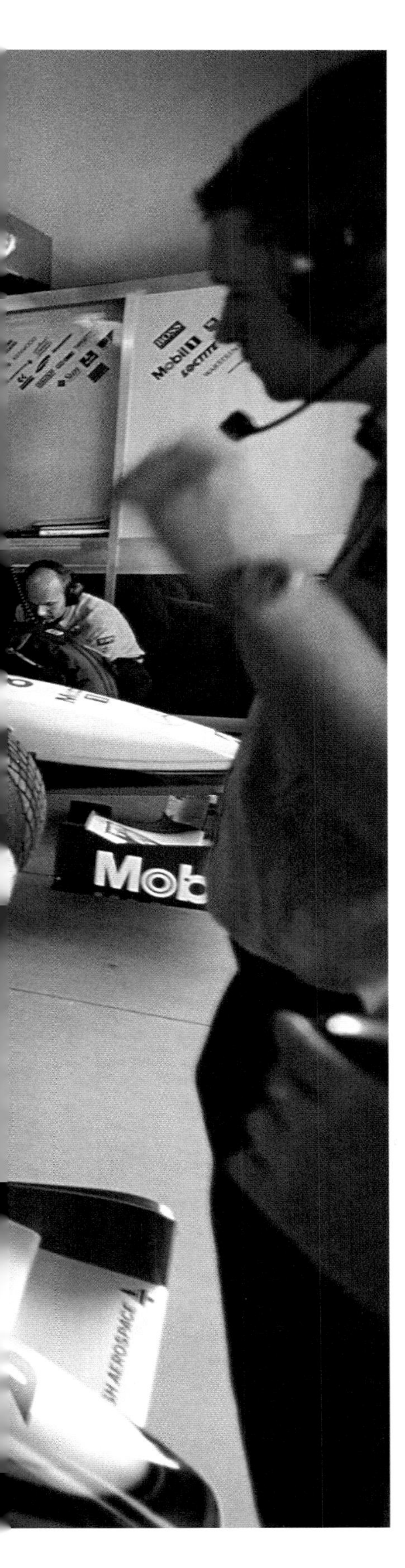

© Hoch Zwei

I don't know if other drivers get as close to their car crew as I do, or if my special feelings for them are because I am particularly lucky to have such a good bunch of guys to work with. They are all highly skilled specialists and the way they go about their jobs, with a bit of banter and a joke, gives an important human dimension to such a mechanical sport.

© Sutton

Above: **Pat Fry, my race engineer, is the man most directly responsible for getting the best out of the number 7 car and its driver**

Left: **West McLaren Mercedes is very much a team effort, with a total of over 300 people working on behalf of the two drivers**

If I don't do a good job I feel I have let the guys down, because they work so hard. It is important to me to have a good relationship with everyone on the team, so I always make a point of going across to the other side of the garage and saying hello to the guys who work on Mika's car.

My race engineer, the man most directly responsible for getting the best out of the car and the driver, is Pat Fry. Our close relationship is very important and I wish we could spend a little more time together socially so I could let Pat know how much I appreciate his efforts. I know that when I have cocked up he knows it, and the reverse is also true. There are no secrets between us. Even in the heat of battle he remains calm and I am fortunate to have such a level-headed guy as my closest associate.

Technically, Pat is a very good engineer and he is also quite good at the human level, particularly when the going gets tough. He knows the things to say to me that are going to remove the doubts I sometimes have. If I am having difficulties he will help quantify how much of it could be the car and how much of it is down to me. He responds positively to every situation, which is very important for maintaining morale.

Pat's assistant is Paul Monaghan, who shares the responsibilities of running my car from the engineering side. Paul is very enthusiastic about his job, which mainly involves working with his computer and drawing the information we need to improve our performance. His nickname is 'Pedals' because he used to design the pedals for the cars. A lot of the guys have nicknames and that is a good thing for fostering team spirit.

Stephen and I have an intimate relationship . . . you get to know someone pretty well when they have to fondle your groin!

The number-one mechanic on my car is Gary 'Wimp' Wheeler, though I always call him Gary because I have respect for my elders. Gary works closely with Peter Vale and Stephen Giles, the number-two mechanics on my car. Peter is called 'Patch' because he has a balding spot on the back of his head and, like most Australians, he is very direct. He is not shy about coming up and expressing his opinion and I appreciate his honesty. If I did well he will say: 'You did a really good job today', or if I didn't: 'What were you doing out there today?' If the car stands still long enough Patch will polish it and I can really relate to the pride he has in his work.

Stephen Giles is another I can relate to, because he trains a lot and is probably the fittest guy on the team. Stephen and I have an intimate relationship because he is the one who helps me get into the cockpit and fasten up my seat belts. You get to know someone pretty well when they have to fondle your groin!

Anton Stipinovich and Julian Chapman spend most of their time working with computers. Anton, whose title is Embedded Systems Engineer, is new to that job on my car and quietly found his way after just a few races. Julian, who works on data analysis and is also new this season, found his niche just as quickly. It can be difficult for newcomers to fit into the race-team crews because they have to earn the respect of those who've been there for a while.

© Hoch Zwei

Stephen Giles is one of the nine guys who works directly on my car. When I'm getting in and out of it he works directly on me

It is comforting for a driver to know his car is prepared by people who are so careful and so dedicated to their jobs

Trevor Lawes, the gearbox technician on my car, has been with the team for many years. Obviously, he loves his work and his racing or he wouldn't put up with all the travel, the long hours and the hardship that goes with being a Grand Prix mechanic. Like the others, Trevor is very conscientious about his work. It is comforting, especially from the safety point of view, for a driver to know his car is prepared by people who are so careful and so dedicated to their jobs.

Derek Jeanes, who is responsible for looking after the fuel for my car, and also does several other jobs, is a very quiet guy and would never come up and talk to you unless you talk to him first, which I often do. I also talk to my tyre man, Steve 'Forks' Morrow. When he's working on the tyres outside the garage I will ask him what's happening and he will give me the low-down and the gossip. Like many of the guys, Forks also works on one of the most critical aspects of a race: the pit stops.

The speed of F1 pit stops these days is determined more by how long refue ling takes than

During a race over twenty of our people perform pit stop duties. They have a reputation for being the best in the business

I really enjoy the teamwork element of a pit stop. It can be an anxious

The speed of F1 pit stops these days is determined more by how long refuelling takes than by how fast four tyres can be taken off and replaced. Our team has a reputation for being one of the quickest and most efficient at refuelling, and that's why I think Forks Morrow, and his partner Patch Vale, deserve special credit. They are both big strong guys

and their size really makes a difference. Patch shoulders the heavy hose while Forks clicks the nozzle onto the car. They very rarely ever make a mistake and knowing these guys are behind you, along with the rest of the approximately twenty people involved in a pit stop, gives you a lot of confidence.

by how fast four tyres can be taken off and replaced

© Hoch Zwei

:ime for us all and to see it come together without a hitch is very satisfying

I really enjoy the teamwork element of a pit stop. It can be an anxious time for us all and to see it come together without a hitch is very satisfying. Mike Negline, the team's chief mechanic and another extremely hard-working and competent guy, handles the lollipop, the sign on a long pole that shows Mika and me when the pit crew have finished their work. It is a fantastic feeling when Mike raises the lollipop and you tear back out onto the track. It is even more rewarding when a quick pit stop helps you win a race, as was the case when I won at Monza in 1997.

I also work closely with Steve Hallam, the senior race engineer, and Dave Ryan, our team manager. Steve controls the team meetings and debriefings, and provides an overview of what happens on a daily basis and in the future. He is the perfect guy for that, so level-

© Hoch Zwei

Thanks to the good work of Forklift, Patch, Gary and the rest of the guys the car can be fitted with fresh tyres and refuelled in about eight seconds

headed, never flustered and always reasoned and methodical in his approach. He is very clear when he delivers his speeches, leaving no room for any doubts. Dave Ryan has been with the team since 1974, and all that experience and his calm temperament make him ideally suited for the complicated job of managing the team. During qualifying Dave helps Pat Fry work with me, pinpointing specific areas we need to work on, and both of them talk to me over the radio during the race.

West
Mobil 1

© Hoch Zwei

Over a race weekend we seem to spend as much time in team briefings as we do in the cars. The excellent engineering minds are a vital ingredient in our success

Friday 8 May

The main objective for me in the Spanish race was to try and capitalize on the momentum I had after Imola, and that was what most of the media people wanted to talk about before we went out on the track. Having closed up on Mika in the standings I was asked to assess my chances in the world championship. I again explained that while some people like to look at the big picture I prefer to take each race as it comes. The best way to win a championship is to win all the races. If that isn't possible, and it isn't these days, the next best thing is to finish each race with as many points as possible. You just have to do the best you can each weekend.

Come the end of the season, it won't make me a failure if I don't win the championship; it will mean only that somebody has scored more points than I did. Although I was now just three points away from Mika, with one quarter of the schedule already over, it was not something that I spent a lot of time analysing. This early in the season the points situation doesn't mean very much. The main thing is to focus on each race and try to get as many points as possible. As it turned out, I got some points in Spain, but fell short of the maximum.

I think the tone for my Spanish weekend was set during the test session at the circuit the previous week. On the second last day of testing I had a fairly hefty accident at the final corner. I lost the back end of the car on some sand that had been dragged onto the track, sailed over a gravel trap that tends not to reduce much speed when you're travelling at about 150 miles an hour, and ploughed into a barrier. I braced my helmet against the side of the car in preparation for the impact, which was quite heavy, and it left me with a slightly sore head.

The main thing is to focus on each race and try to get as many points as possible

Up to that point I was very comfortable with the car. The guys rebuilt it for me and I was back on form physically the next day. I got a couple of runs in but it started to rain so we had to pack it up before we had a chance to perfect the set-up. Mika, meanwhile, had run through his full test programme and it was his set-up that I used to start practice on the race weekend. I wasn't very comfortable with it and although I reverted back to my own set-up later, vital time had been lost by starting off on the wrong foot. From that point on I was struggling. I just never got on top of things to the point where I had full confidence in the car.

It was a complete reversal of the situation at Imola, where Mika was struggling. Here, we were still at the top of the timesheets, but he was ahead. From the first practice run I was having difficulty in the braking areas and that was where Mika was gaining the time.

Saturday 9 May

On Saturday morning I lost half an hour's practice because I spun off and put the car into a gravel trap. In qualifying, my best lap was good enough for second on the grid, but seven tenths slower than Mika's pole time.

I congratulated Mika on his good lap, but I was disappointed with my performance in comparison. It was one of those occasions when he was at one with his car and I wasn't. This situation seemed to swing between us from circuit to circuit. The margin between us comes down to the confidence of the driver in being able to extract all the performance from his car. Mika had done that from the start of the weekend and right from the word go I don't think I got my act together. I lacked the confidence to attack the track. On every Grand Prix circuit you have to be able to hit the corners knowing what you want to do with the car. It's no good wondering what the car is going to do. It is as simple as that. Now I would have to try to get the set-up more to my liking in the warm-up before the race.

It was going to be difficult to suddenly find the form I hadn't been able to achieve in the first two days. But I was certainly going to try. A race is always very different to qualifying because it is all about being consistent over a number of laps, to state the obvious, and

I had been pretty comfortable with my race performances so far. There is a good run down to the first corner on this circuit, so there would be an opportunity to try to transform the positions within the first lap. If I was successful at that, then the whole race would look quite different.

Sunday 10 May

Opposite: **With Mika alone in the lead it was left to me to be best of the rest in Spain. It was satisfying to do that, and to know that I'd given everything I had**

Mika and I were first and second again in the warm-up. The guys worked hard on my car, making adjustments to the set-up, trying to help me find that last little bit that would help me click into the circuit. The car felt very nervous at the rear and was oversteering too much for my liking. We were still working on it on the starting grid. It is never a good sign when a driver is still trying to play catch-up at this late stage, and at the start I was feeling neither comfortable nor confident.

Mika won the drag race to the first corner, I was second and that was basically that. It would be extremely difficult to change our running order on a circuit where overtaking is so difficult because of the several fast turns where you lose downforce when you are following another car closely.

Mika won the drag race to the first corner, I was second and that was basically that

But I was absolutely determined to avoid making what was really only an average weekend for me into a bad weekend. I had to stay on the road, but I pushed very hard and never gave up. In fact, I believe I drove slightly harder in Barcelona than I had at Imola, or at any of the previous races. My attitude here was that I'm more than fit enough to drive every lap at the maximum, so why not do it? For my own satisfaction I had to know that I'd given absolutely everything I had, and I believe I did that.

My Spanish Grand Prix was really just a battle with myself, because there were no close challengers behind me and there was no way I could challenge Mika. Well done to him, I said. That weekend he gave me a bit of a driving lesson.

© Sutton
© Sutton

Marlb

POTENZA

the monaco grand prix

monte carlo, 24 may

Shell

Wednesday 20 May

My 'second home' Grand Prix is unusual in several ways, beginning with the fact that the weekend starts with the first day's practice on Thursday instead of Friday. This tradition is supposed to give the local residents a chance to go about their normal affairs on Friday. Since the whole place is closed off for the Grand Prix anyway, it amounts to a four-day race weekend, especially for the drivers. The Monaco Grand Prix is the glamour event of the year for the sponsors and when we're not in the car we spend a lot of the time running around with our public relations hats on instead of our helmets.

I love living here. Monaco is small and comfortable, safe, quiet and easy to get around – except on the Grand Prix weekend. The scenery is great and the weather is usually good, certainly compared to my native land. There are some great places to eat and drink in town, and all along the whole Mediterranean coastline. The locals don't bother you because they are so used to seeing famous sportsmen. We all lead normal lives, do the shopping and the washing up, pay the bills. Several drivers live here and some of us socialize together. I see Jacques Villeneuve quite a bit, and sometimes Johnny Herbert and Alex Wurz.

There are practical reasons for drivers basing themselves in Monaco, tax advantages being one of them. With racing, testing, sponsor functions and other events, I have to do about a hundred flights a year. Monaco is centrally located for most destinations and the Nice airport is only thirty minutes away from my flat. I am only about an hour and three quarters away from London and about two hours from Scotland. It works both ways, in that friends can easily come and visit.

Monaco is an amazing place for a Grand Prix. It seems weird driving an F1 car on the streets where you go shopping, and every time I go out I think it is crazy to be racing in such ridiculously confined circumstances. But it is also very exciting and I would never want to lose this race.

Monaco is a great place to live, and an amazing place for a Grand Prix. It's crazy to go racing in such confined circumstances. I love it!

The circuit is the ultimate challenge for a driver's mind. Mentally, you're on edge the whole time, concentrating so hard that your head hurts. I don't think there is any other track in the world that is as stressful. It is a question of taking your car to the absolute limit and keeping it there, without actually going over the limit. If you do happen to exceed that limit slightly you have to be able to get your car back into shape in a split-second. There is simply no room for error.

I don't think there is any other track in the world that is as stressful. It is a question of taking your car to the absolute limit and keeping it there

I felt a little apprehensive about pushing hard on a track where if you make the slightest mistake you hit the barriers and risk damaging the car. But I also felt that I would be competitive enough to win here – and I needed to be. I ought to have won more than one race by now and it still irked me when I thought about Australia and Argentina, the two races I was in a position to win and didn't. Those disappointments were offset by the victory at Imola, which was great for my morale. It was high time I won again.

Thursday 21 May

Braking on the entry to corners is more critical here than anywhere else, so in the first practice sessions I was experimenting with establishing the braking points. My experiments led to a couple of excursions down the escape road at Ste Devote, the first corner of the lap. However, I managed to avoid contact with the barriers and at the end of practice I was third, less than a second behind Mika, who was quickest. I hadn't quite got the balance of the car to my liking – it felt a bit loose at the rear end – but there were no major problems in the handling department.

© Sutton

Friday 22 May

A busy day of off-track obligations included making several public relations appearances, meeting sponsors, chatting to fans and signing autographs, attending meetings with the team and hosting a lunch for members of the British press.

A prominent question posed by the journalists concerned the continuing debate, at least the one being conducted in the press, over my future with the team. The old rumour about Michael Schumacher coming to McLaren had not gone away. I told them that I had been assured that my position was safe as long as we, both myself and the team, continued our current form.

The circuit is the ultimate challenge for a driver's mind. Mentally, you're on the edge the whole time, concentrating so hard your head hurts

Opposite: **A qualifying lap is a trip into the unknown, looking for the edge. Finding it, without hitting anything, is a wonderfully thrilling sensation**

At the point you are going into one corner, you are already planning how to tackle the mid-corner and the exit

Generally, I am on good terms with the members of the press, especially the British division, which naturally tends to focus more on British drivers. If there is one criticism of their treatment of drivers it is that some journalists go to extremes. When you do well they praise you too much and when you do less well, or even have an average weekend, they dish out more dirt than is warranted. I know that editors often want sensational news to sell more papers, so I try to keep an open mind about what is written.

Later that evening, when I had some time to myself back in the flat, I thought about Saturday's qualifying session and the kind of lap I wanted to do. Pole was my goal because it is more difficult to overtake here than anywhere else we race.

Before attempting a quick lap you have to clear your mind of any distractions, and focus completely on the task at hand. The track is very short, not much over two miles, but all the twists and turns, many of them blind from the driver's point of view, make it extremely complicated. Visualizing the lap before you attempt it is a very important part of the preparation. You have to get your mind in gear for what you are expecting to do: braking points, gear changes, acceleration and so on.

A completely flat-out qualifying lap at Monaco is a very strange experience. When you are speeding extremely quickly between the narrow barriers it is almost as if you are not consciously aware that you are doing it. It's a kind of out-of-body sensation, as if you're watching yourself do it. Everything comes at you and passes by you in a rush, while you're also anticipating the on-coming rushes. At the point you are going into one corner, you are already planning how to tackle the mid-corner and the exit, and also thinking about how you want to position yourself to take the next corner. At the time, when you are at one with the car, you have to be operating at an extremely high level of awareness. But when reality comes back, after you've done it, it's actually quite difficult to comprehend what happened. It seems to have all taken place at a subconscious level.

In a qualifying lap you are going quicker than you ever have before. It is the quickest lap you will do all weekend, and even after many previous practice laps a blinding qualifying lap is a new experience. You don't know what it is going to feel like until you hit the edge. It's a wonderfully thrilling sensation, a bit like kissing a girl for the first time!

Saturday 23 May

In morning practice I ended up posting the second quickest time, before my continuing experiments to find an even faster way around Monaco led to an unwanted confrontation with a barrier in the last part of the swimming-pool section. On previous laps I had been able to

COMPUTER
ASSOCIATES

Opposite: **Monaco is traditionally an unpredictable race, where anything can happen and often does**

carry more speed through here than Mika, and I thought I would see just how far I could push it. Unfortunately, my over-exuberance led to a spin, to the detriment of the rear wing, which was ripped off, and the rear suspension, which was slightly bent. Fortunately, the blow was cushioned by the tyres stacked in front of the steel barriers at this point on the circuit and there wasn't a lot of repair work for the guys to do.

You have to be really careful here with backmarkers, and also take care to avoid other people's accidents

In the afternoon I qualified second on the grid, just three tenths of a second behind Mika's pole time. Much of the difference between us came down to traffic, which is always a problem here. I was delayed by other cars on two of the four runs I made. In fact, as I was leaving the pitlane to go out on one of my qualifying runs I nearly ran into the back of Riccardo Rosset's Tyrrell, because he decided to brake right at the exit of the pitlane. Thankfully, he came off his brakes just when I thought, Shit! This is impact time. How do I explain this one to the team?

You have to be really careful here with backmarkers, and also take care to avoid other people's accidents. One lap I had to abort because Rubens Barrichello crashed his Stewart at the Rascasse hairpin. On my last run, potentially my quickest, I came up behind Jacques Villeneuve's Williams and was frustrated when he held me up. Later, when I saw he had qualified back in thirteenth place, I realized he was obviously having car problems and felt less angry.

There was nothing wrong with my car and the two clear laps I had, my first and third runs, were both good enough for provisional pole. Of course, I would have preferred to be on the actual pole, but it wasn't to be, and I would still start from the front row. I consoled myself with the knowledge that the outcome of the race on a track where overtaking is so rare can be decided by superior pit-stop strategy. Monaco

DOCTOR
West
7

© Sutton

is traditionally also an unpredictable race, where anything can happen and often does.

Another tradition on the social calendar are the pre-race Saturday night functions, many of them held on the suitably over the top yachts that crowd the harbour, or the larger liners anchored beyond it. To attend one of these, on behalf of our sponsor West, Heidi and I were taken on a tender for a trip through heavy seas to a big ship outside the harbour. Coming alongside we were tossed about like a cork on the ocean. It was quite nerve-racking and we must have looked a bit white-faced and shaken when we finally got on board.

Playing about with boats is another Monaco tradition. Heidi and I sailed to a couple of functions and I took a turn at the wheel of a rather grand yacht

Another tradition on the social calendar are the pre-race Saturday night functions

It was a lot calmer back in the harbour, where we joined a Mobil function on board a fantastic new yacht called *The Iroquois*. That night we had a very pleasant evening on the yacht with some old friends, including Ken McCulloch, a well-known Scot and the owner of the Malmaison restaurants and hotels.

Sunday 24 May

In the warm-up, running with quite heavy fuel loads, Mika and I posted the first and third fastest times. I knew it was going to be extremely unlikely that I could beat a guy in the same car into Ste Devote corner, so my opening strategy would be to stay on my team-mate's gearbox and wait for developments.

We made equally good starts. On the way round Ste Devote I tried to squeeze past Mika but ran out of space. So I slotted in behind him and dropped back a bit to assess the situation. To avoid trouble I was very conservative over the

MIL
SEVEN
West

first couple of laps, then settled down quite comfortably into matching the brisk pace being set by Mika. We quickly pulled away from the rest of the field. I had no trouble staying with him, keeping the pressure on and confident that if any mistakes were made they weren't going to be mine. We were both driving flat out, and between lap 4 and lap 12, as our fuel loads lightened, we traded fastest race laps a dozen times. Five laps later my race was over.

From the beginning I sat on Mika's tail. We were both driving flat out and were soon streets ahead of the rest

On the way round Ste Devote I tried to squeeze past Mika but ran out of space

There was no advance warning for the engine failure that locked up the rear axle as I was coming out of the Loewes tunnel on the approach to the chicane. The car slewed left and right before I was able to straighten it out and coast to a halt up the escape road.

On the long walk back to the pits spectators offered me their condolences. A group of English fans had a tray of beer, so I asked one of them if I could have a drink. He said sure, but his wife would never believe that he had had a beer with a famous racing driver. I said I was no different from him, especially since I was now also a spectator at the Monaco Grand Prix.

As our fuel loads lightened we traded fastest race laps a dozen times. Five laps later my race was over . . .

So I had a couple of sips of beer to drown my sorrows and sat there for about ten minutes watching the other cars go by, thinking about what might have been. It was hugely disappointing. After having been so hyped up and concentrating so hard the abrupt end to my race was a shock to the system. Gradually, as the adrenalin level went down, I felt quite calm again. I was able to come to terms with my fate and by the time I got back to the pits I was singing the old song: 'Well, that's racing.'

There was no advance warning for the engine failure that brought me to a smoking halt at the exit from the tunnel

© Sutton

After the race, which Mika won handily, Heidi and I went back to the flat to get ready for Prince Rainier's traditional post-race gala dinner. Heidi put on a smart frock and looked like the beautiful model she is. I got all dressed up in a kilt and looked like the dour Scot I felt. After the dinner we went to a nightclub where most of the team was gathered. Jacques Villeneuve came in and we met up with some other friends. We chatted and danced a bit, but called it a night relatively early because Heidi was working the next day and I was travelling to a test session at Monza. Going straight back to work, and focusing on the next race, in Canada, was the best way to get the 1998 Monaco Grand Prix out of my mind.

The abrupt end was a shock to the system. After drowning my sorrows I was able to come to terms with my fate and put it down to bad racing luck

the
canadian
grand prix
montreal, 7 june
WARSTEINER
FF
7
R-7

On the Monday after Monaco, on our way to Monza for a week's testing, Mika, Ron Dennis and I went down to a small circuit near Marseilles where we filmed a TV commercial for the new 'A'-class Mercedes road car. This was something different, a bit of fun after my disappointment in the Grand Prix; and, unlike the race, since we were shooting to a prepared script there was no unhappy ending for me. I was in better shape for the filming than my team-mate because Mika had thoroughly celebrated his win and was feeling a bit second-hand.

Heidi and I were happy to visit Montreal, one of the best cities on the F1 tour. It was a perfect weekend, while it lasted

The Monza test was a general one to prepare the cars for Canada, and we also did some tyre testing for Bridgestone. Even though we experienced a couple of engine problems at the test I wasn't particularly worried about it happening again in a race because Mario Illien was there. Mario is the design genius at Ilmor Engineering, the company that produces our Mercedes engines. We talked a lot during the test. Speaking to him was reassuring, though it was a bit disconcerting to hear from him that the faulty part that caused my engine problem in Monaco was made in Scotland. I wouldn't have minded so much if it was made anywhere else in the world, especially in England!

Anyway, with Mario on the job I could put engines out of my mind and concentrate on my goal for Canada, which was not to make any mistakes in the race and gain back some of the seventeen-point lead Mika had over me. Unfortunately, when your team enjoys an advantage over the opposition and you are able to run one-two the way we can, the winner can only gain four points at a time. The winner gets ten points and the second-place finisher gets six. Of course, there was always the possibility I would get maximum points and Mika would get none if he didn't finish, but that would not be good for the team. As a driver, you always have to balance out your personal championship ambitions with the team's main goal, which is to win the Constructors' Championship.

After the test I went home for a couple of days, then flew to Montreal on Sunday. The

fact that I had very nearly won the Canadian race in 1997, and probably would have except for an electrical problem, gave me more confidence. As it turned out, my confidence was well placed. Everything worked nearly perfectly over the three days . . . nearly perfectly.

Friday 5 June

In the first hour of practice Mika and I were quickest and had trouble-free sessions from a technical point of view at Le Circuit Gilles Villeneuve. We were both pushing very hard and in the second hour I had a couple of off-course excursions. On one of them I went straight on at the chicane before the pits, ran over a marker cone and knocked off the car's front wing. Meanwhile, Mika had a couple of spins and also slid into a guard rail. It was interesting to note that his problems were in the tricky first corner, where you have to brake hard, turn sharp left, then negotiate a tight right-hander. Since this was one place on the circuit where I felt very comfortable it gave me a bit more confidence for qualifying.

© Hoch Zwei/Kunkel

Though we were in the French-speaking part of Canada, my business manager Iain Cunningham and I spoke in Scottish

In the evening Heidi and I went out with her parents, her brother and his fiancée, my friend David Cawthorne and my business manager Iain Cunningham for a relaxing dinner at a restaurant close to my hotel. Our guests were James and Jeanne-Claude Strong. James is

Chief Executive Officer of Qantas Airways and was in Montreal for a meeting of the airline organization, IATA. Over the last few years Iain and I had come to know James and his Qantas team quite well and we had an enjoyable evening talking about the airline business, motor racing and motorbikes. Both James and Jeanne-Claude are keen motorcyclists and good friends of the Australian world champion rider Michael Doohan, who is a neighbour of mine in Monaco. So we had plenty to talk about and we all agreed it would be a fine thing next March if James could present me with the winner's trophy at the 1999 Qantas Australia Grand Prix!

Saturday 6 June

Morning practice finished with Mika and me setting exactly the same times – an absolute dead heat and a very rare occurrence that showed how evenly matched we were. Again, I went off course a couple of times but there were no particular worries because I was experimenting with lines and looking for the latest possible braking points. It is normal to see how much you can get away with in the last practice session before qualifying.

After very nearly winning the 1997 Canadian Grand Prix I was determined to pull out all the stops and finish the job this year

© Sutton

Since a win in this race was so important for my championship it made getting pole position even more vital and to prepare for it mentally I tried something different. I believe very much in visualizing, trying to get a clear picture in your mind of exactly what you want

West

© Hoch Zwei/Kunkel

to do all the way around the track – in this case a quick qualifying lap. This time, with the help of my trainer Jerry Powell, I also applied some of the power of positive thinking that many people believe in.

As time ran out in qualifying I concentrated on thinking positively about pushing to the absolute limit to get pole position

While we were in Canada Jerry talked to an athlete who has competed successfully in triathlons, the incredibly exhausting sport where you punish yourself in consecutive events by swimming, riding a bicycle for miles and then finishing off the day by running a marathon. This chap believes the key to success is all in your mind and that by thinking positive thoughts you can convince your body to do things it normally would not do. I am not necessarily a believer in everything fitness gurus have to say but one of his pieces of advice sounded appropriate. He told Jerry that to succeed in a goal you should tell yourself that you deserve it. Since my goal was pole position, and I was prepared to throw everything I had into it, why shouldn't I get the reward I deserved? I thought it was worth a try.

We had decided we were going to wait until the very last minute for me to do my last run

Jerry said later that before my last qualifying run I sat for nearly four minutes in the car in the garage, thinking those positive thoughts and visualizing what I had to do. I never realized it was that long, but there was extra time available because in discussions with Dave Ryan and Pat Fry we had decided we were going to wait until the very last minute for me to do my last run. We felt that the grip on the track would improve steadily and the idea was that I would literally come across the finish line when the chequered flag came out to end the session.

After my first two runs I was quickest, while Mika, having made some mistakes and been held up by slower traffic, had aborted his runs and not yet even qualified. When he went out again and got a clear lap he put in a best time that was 0.062 seconds faster than mine. As the clock ran down

To get pole is such a release of emotion because you know you're well on the way to realizing the goal for the weekend: winning the race

towards the end of the hour I sat there in the car with my eyes closed, visualizing the dozen or so corners that lay ahead and pondering some of the things Jerry had told me. When the time came to go out I remember driving down the pitlane and thinking, 'Well, I'm a fairly decent bloke and I do deserve this pole position!' It's funny how the mind works.

At the first split mark, about a third of the way around the circuit, I was 0.3 seconds ahead of the time Mika had achieved. Then I screwed up in the middle section and lost all that advantage. I got a wee bit out of shape in turns six

It was difficult to describe how happy I was to get pole

and seven, running wide on the entry, and had to hesitate putting the power on. It's horrible when that happens – you see the split time on the dashboard read-out and you know you've only got a couple of places left on the track to get it back. I had to put something extra into that last section. It was here that the experimenting I had done in practice paid off. I took a gamble at the last corner before the pits and pushed to the absolute limit, and on the exit the car came right out to within a few centimetres of the wall. When I crossed the finish line under the chequered flag my time was 0.069 seconds better than Mika's.

Even then I had difficulty believing that pole was actually mine and asked for confirmation on the radio. It may seem ridiculous, but even when I have won a race, halfway around the slowing down lap and after I have been punching the air with excitement, I get back on the radio and say: 'Would you mind please confirming that I have actually won the race?' I guess I am worried about having drifted into a dream – maybe a nightmare, like drifting into a gravel trap – and being brought back to reality.

This time, after I was assured my dream was true, it was difficult to describe how happy I was to get pole. Back in the garage the whole team seemed as pleased as I was and it was a bit uncomfortable to have to share our joy in public.

© Hoch Zwei/Kunkel

I would prefer to have had a few private moments alone with the guys, without all the TV cameras, journalists and photographers there to record it all. No matter how much you put into it as a driver, your results are always part of a team effort and you want to be able to look each other in the eye, shake hands and say well done, away from outsiders. I know it is part of the sport and that the media wants to capture all the emotion, and believe me there is a lot of it in our team, but when I am aware we are being watched so closely I may not react as positively and as whole-heartedly as I would if we could just have a few moments alone.

This, the eighth pole position of my career, was more exciting for me than some of the earlier ones I had with the Williams team in 1995. Then, we also had a car that had the potential to win and I was always a little embarrassed at the extra attention that came your way when you were fastest in qualifying. But now, after a couple of seasons when our McLarens were less competitive, I am fully aware of how fortunate we are to have cars capable of getting pole, and more. I wish championship points were awarded for being quickest in qualifying, as well as for the race results, and these days they are certainly closely related. To get pole is such a release of emotion because you know that you're almost half way to realizing the goal for the weekend: winning the race. I slept well that night.

Before the pole lap I had visualized what I had to do. Then I replayed it for the benefit of anyone who would listen!

Sunday 7 June

After the warm-up session, when the car felt good on full tanks, we decided to stay with our decision to stop only once in the race for fuel and fresh tyres. Starting with a heavier load of fuel made my early priorities straightforward. I would need to get away quickly and smoothly, avoid making any mistakes and hold the opposition behind me in the early laps until I could burn off some fuel and speed up.

Everything went according to plan, except that I had to repeat the process three times. At the start there was a big accident behind me. Several cars crashed in the first corner and the red flags were brought out to stop the race. It was a frightening situation, with the

Benetton of Alexander Wurz somersaulting through the air, but fortunately nobody was hurt and there was a full grid again when we got ready to take off for the second time.

Normally the few moments before the start of a Grand Prix is a very serious time, but on this occasion there was an amusing incident. On the first start I had lined my car up at a slight angle in the pole position, so I could have a straighter run down to the first corner. After we had lined up on the grid again for the re-start Dave Ryan was told by the FIA Race Director Charlie Whiting that information from the race office showed I had jumped the first start. This could have been very bad news if the race had gone on, because I might have been assessed a ten-second penalty.

I think what happened was that the sensor that is buried in the track at each grid position picked up an early movement because my car was at an angle. I was thankful to get

At the start everything went according to plan, except I had to repeat the process three times

I was able to fend off Michael's challenges and felt in complete control of the race

© Sutton

a second chance and this time I had the car in its proper position. As we were sitting there I looked up at the starting gantry where Charlie Whiting was and gave him the thumbs-up. I don't think he expected the polesitter to take time out for a bit of fun at this crucial moment. Charlie looked very surprised, then started laughing and gave me a thumbs-up signal in return.

When Charlie sent us away again everything went well from my point of view, but behind

me there was more trouble: another collision involving several cars in the first corner. This time, the Safety Car came onto the circuit and as the race leader it was my job to lead the field around behind it for several laps while the mess was cleaned up.

We started racing again on the sixth lap, although I was now the one representative of our team. When the race was re-started the first time Mika had trouble with his gearbox and his Canadian Grand Prix was over. You have a more secure feeling in the lead when you know

Michael was all over me like a rash, especially on the straights

Right: **The mechanical problem that caused my retirement was a terrible disappointment**

your team-mate is behind to back you up, but as it turned out I had no trouble keeping Michael Schumacher's Ferrari at bay.

Michael was all over me like a rash, especially on the straights, where his lighter fuel load gave him a top-speed boost. I wasn't concerned because with every lap my fuel load was lightening and my speed went up accordingly. I was able to fend off Michael's challenges and felt in complete control of the race.

On lap 13 the Safety Car made another appearance, this time because a car had gone off course and on its return dragged a large quantity of dirt onto the track surface. After a couple of laps behind the Safety Car while the dirt was swept away we were again in racing mode and again I was in charge of the Canadian Grand Prix.

As I went past the pits on the nineteenth lap the car started losing power. I immediately got on the radio and informed the team that something was wrong and as I was speaking the power went right down to the point that the engine wouldn't do much more than idle. I

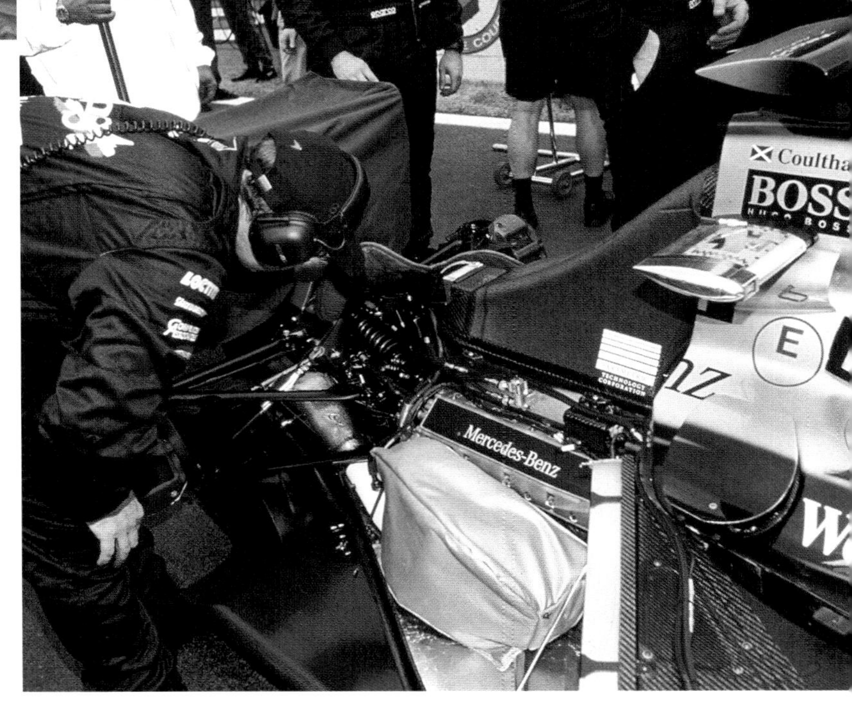

coasted around for the rest of the lap and drove straight into the garage. As it turned out, there was nothing wrong with the engine. A bolt had fallen out of the throttle linkage so that even with my foot to the floor the engine was unable to respond.

It was a terrible disappointment, an emotion that I was unfortunately experiencing too often. Perhaps that's why my initial feelings of being desperately frustrated were quickly displaced by the positive memories of having responded to the pressure of what had been a crucial weekend for me. I went out and got pole position when I had to. I was in control of the race and the failure to win it had nothing to do with me. There was no question in my mind that I was up

© Sutton

The team and Heidi consoled me. At least I had responded to the challenges with a performance that couldn't be questioned

© Hoch Zwei/Kunkel

to the job, because I had done everything I had to do. That was important for my confidence, and also for the team's confidence in me.

From the championship point of view our non-finishes in Montreal meant Mika's lead over me was unchanged, but Michael Schumacher went on to win the race and was now five points ahead of me. This was a bit worrying because if I fell too far behind Mika and Michael kept driving a wedge between us the team might have to start concentrating on Mika's championship. But as far as we were concerned it was still a two-horse race between the McLaren team-mates, and my job was to get back in front of Michael and close the gap to Mika as soon as possible.

David Coul
Powered b
Mercedes-Be
Mc

the french grand prix

magny cours, 28 June

© Sutton

© Sutton

In the interval between the races in Canada and France we tested at Silverstone and then at Magny Cours, site of the French race. On the weekend between the tests I flew to Florida for the christening of Gil and Angela de Ferran's daughter Anna. As Anna's godfather I felt it was important to be there and to be able to participate in a happy social event gave me a chance to sample more of the normal life that is so difficult for an F1 driver to get, especially one who is fighting for the world championship.

Including the French Grand Prix there were nine races to go – nine races to win. With ninety points to play for, my championship situation could easily turn around. Obviously, clawing back Mika's advantage was going to be quite difficult because we had the same cars. But in the same way that after seven races he had a seventeen-point lead, it could turn around and go the other way for me. So I just had to focus on

In the seven races so far the driver of the number 7 car had more than his share of bad luck. Surely it would change for the better in France

© Collins/Sutton

My classic Mercedes 280SL is a prized possession. It's almost exactly the same age as me, so it needs lots of tender loving care

each race instead of the points total. I wasn't going to lose any sleep over what had happened in the past. I needed to change what would happen in the future.

I also needed a reliability call in my favour. Mika and I both had two non-finishes because of reliability problems. Meanwhile, Ferrari's reliability had been impressive and both Michael and Eddie Irvine had capitalized on it to move closer to us in the team standings. This was good for F1, because the rivalry between the two most successful teams in the sport's history kept the interest high, but it was worrying for us.

Friday 26 June

Our cars had performed well in the test at Magny Cours, particularly in several long runs, so I was confident about being able to go well in race conditions. To start the weekend the main thing to work on was preparing the set-up to get the maximum out of the car in qualifying.

© Sutton

My McLaren MP4/13 needs servicing, too, and pit stops would influence the outcome of my French Grand Prix

In the first hour of practice I had a slight edge over Mika. In the final session I fell back to third fastest, behind Eddie Irvine's Ferrari. I lost most of the time because of a slight problem with the rear brakes locking going into one corner. Nonetheless, I was as quick as Mika in all the sectors around the track, so going for pole was still a viable proposition. It was obvious that grid positions were going to be very important because the first six cars in practice were separated by less than a second on the timesheets.

Saturday 27 June

At the end of the day the qualifying session classification timesheet showed that the first six cars were again separated by less than a second. Unfortunately, the times also showed that I remained in the same place as I had been on Friday. Mika was on pole, Michael was second and I was third. For the first time this season I was off the front row of the starting grid.

I was desperately hoping to challenge for pole but in truth I was never in contention

My trouble began in morning practice, when I got a bit frustrated trying to find a traffic-free lap and slid off into a gravel trap. This setback, which left me fourth fastest in practice, lost me valuable time that would otherwise have been spent perfecting the set-up, and also interfered with building up the steady rhythm you need to get into qualifying mode.

I was desperately hoping to challenge for pole but in truth I was never in contention. At one point even my third place was being threatened by Eddie Irvine. There were three corners that I really struggled with and that is where I lost the time. They were all slow corners and they were the key to a quick lap. I felt there was an instability in the rear end of the car, which meant that I just couldn't carry the speed on the entries to the slower corners. High-speed corners, changes of direction in the chicanes – I was pretty much there in terms of speed. But even from third place on the grid it was still possible to get a good result – even win the race. And that is what I intended to try to do.

Sunday 28 June

In the warm-up I was quickest, ahead of Mika and Michael. This was encouraging and in my mind's eye I saw myself making a perfect start, passing Michael and then challenging Mika, whose overall championship concerns I felt would tend to make him less aggressive. Of course, my positive mental imagery did not include the reality of the negative circumstances that followed.

To begin with, the French Grand Prix was stopped a few seconds after it started. A car stalled on the grid and we had to do it all over again. On the re-start Mika, whose pole position was directly in front of me, faltered slightly and I had to back off. This enabled Michael and Eddie to slip through into a one-two Ferrari formation, which is where they finished. Any chance I might have had to change this result was wiped out by the problems I had in my pit stops.

I was scheduled to stop twice. Before the afternoon was over I made four visits to the

© Sutton

The highlight of my day was a daring move into a momentary second place. Unfortunately, the cameras missed the brilliant overtaking manoeuvre!

pits, where I spent an agonizingly long period of time. My best memory of the approximately ninety-five minutes it took me to complete the race came before my first stop. For several laps I had been stalking Eddie Irvine, whom I was determined to relieve of third place. The opportunity came when he was slipstreaming a slower car down the straight, then pulled alongside to overtake it going into turn 4. We were going flat out down the straight and as the backmarker moved over to give Eddie room I took a deep breath and dived out of Eddie's slipstream into the small gap between the two of them.

Out of the corner of my eye I remember catching a glimpse of the board informing us that only 100 yards remained in which to brake for the corner.

We were three abreast, and at a place where such a manoeuvre was just barely possible, I used my momentum to overtake both cars and braked for the corner at the last possible instant. I thought it was such a brilliant accomplishment that I switched on the radio and let out a 'Whoopee!' The team didn't know what I was exclaiming about because the main TV cameras hadn't caught it. I would love to see a replay of a move that I was so committed to making. It was a big risk and could have ended in tears, so it was very satisfying actually to pull it off successfully.

Since Mika had spun just before this my major move on Eddie effectively put me into second place, though it only lasted for the rest of that lap because the team, unaware of my manoeuvre, called me in for my first stop earlier than was scheduled. The strategy was to call me in early to give me more fuel so I could go longer in the second stint in order to pass Eddie, which, unbeknownst to them, I had already done. As I sat in the pits quietly fuming about my fate it seemed the refuelling was taking longer than usual. I didn't want to say anything on the radio at this critical time because the guys on the pit crew would hear it and might lose concentration. It became obvious there was some kind of difficulty with my refuelling, and when I went back out Pat Fry confirmed there was a problem and that they were working to fix it before my next stop.

The refuelling problems left me fuming at the delay. The guys in the pit crew felt as badly as I did, though it wasn't their fault

© Tap/Hoch Zwei

After the fourth and final pit stop I was able to push hard and salvage a single point from a troubled afternoon

I don't mind admitting that I was very angry when I went back out on the track. To take the risk of overtaking Eddie, gain the advantage, then lose it all was aggravating in the extreme. I had pitted in second place and came out fourth. I kept wanting to flick on the radio and share my frustration but that good little guy that sits on my shoulder kept reminding me that complaining would not really help. I knew the team was doing the best it could. But bottling up my anger may have actually helped me fight back against the adversity I faced in this race. Sometimes it's difficult to concentrate for an hour and a half, especially when things are going well. In this case, with anger added to the adrenalin, my attention never wavered. I drove harder than ever and on the fifty-ninth of the seventy-one laps I set the fastest lap of the race, partly because by that time I was more frustrated than ever.

On lap 55 I came in for my second stop. This time there was a further delay because the 'cat flap' – the cover of the fuel tank opening on the side of the car – was stuck. When they got it open Forks Morrow, the nozzleman, had trouble getting the nozzle to go on. Time and again Forks tried it, but it just would not engage properly. It was an awful feeling to just sit there and watch the other cars go by. Finally, to avoid wasting any more time they sent me out to do another lap while they changed over to Mika's fuel rig. When I came in again Mika's rig wasn't set correctly so we weren't able to get enough fuel in for me to complete the race. After this stop I was back in seventh place and out of the points, so I pushed really hard, overtook two cars and was up to fifth place when I had to come in again. This stop, on lap 63, was just a splash and dash, giving me enough fuel to do the final eight laps, but it dropped me down to eighth. Again I drove as hard as I could and just managed to get sixth place, and a single point, on the last lap of the race.

This was my third mechanical problem in a row and I'm afraid my frustration got the better of me after the race

I felt badly for Forks Morrow, who was very upset about the refuelling fiasco. After the race he came up to me and I could see he wanted to say something. But he didn't have to say a word, because we are all in this together. He doesn't give me a bollocking when I put the car in the gravel, or overshoot the pit stop markers and make it difficult for him to get the nozzle on. So I told Forks that he does his job extremely well, that this was not his problem and he should not worry about it. I thanked him for his good work and we left it at that.

In fact, it wasn't his fault at all. We found out later that the problems were caused by a malfunction of the refuelling equipment and not a human error. Without question Forks and the pit crew are major keys to McLaren's success. In the 1997 Italian Grand Prix at Monza their quick work, especially by Forks on the nozzle, was directly responsible for my winning the race.

Nonetheless, this was my third mechanical problem in a row and I'm afraid my frustration got the better of me after the race. Normally, I believe you should calm down and not let your emotions show but having only got sixth place when second seemed a sure thing left me feeling rather bitter. In the heat of the moment I said to some journalists that what happened was Keystone Cops stuff and not good enough in a World Championship campaign.

Later, I was able to rationalize it more reasonably and put it down to the luck of racing. It just hadn't gone my way. For that matter, the French Grand Prix was bad luck for the whole team, because the Ferraris of Michael and Eddie finished first and second, while Mika was third. If the race had started the first time, and without my refuelling problem, we could have had the one-two finish. Now, Ferrari was just eleven points away from us in the Constructors' Championship. In the drivers' standings Michael was fourteen points ahead of me, and just four behind Mika, while I was twenty points – two wins away – from Mika.

7
Mobil
1

Mid-term Report

At this, the halfway point in the season, the hard facts in the drivers' standings were hard to face, but I felt they were not an accurate reflection of my performances. In the past three consecutive races circumstances beyond my control left me with only a single point to show for a lot of hard work. Overall, despite being as competitive as anybody in the field, I had only a single win in the first eight races. This was simply not right. It was impossible that it could keep going on like this; the law of averages would surely not allow it. It had to change, and I was going to do everything in my power to make it change. Racing on even terms I knew I could beat both Mika and Michael. There was no way I was going to back off and I resolved that in the remainder of the season anyone who wanted to win the driving title was going to have to beat me to do it.

The hectic battle for the driving title brought me into the limelight more than at any time in my career

Being in a position to fight for the championship had brought me into the limelight more than at any time in my racing career. There was increased attention from the press, and some of the questions I was being asked made it apparent that my realistic approach to my job was not what the more sensational side of the media wanted. I am very aware of the fact that I would be a better bet from a journalistic point of view if I was prepared to say things like: 'That was the best lap of my life!' or 'That was the biggest shunt of my life!' or 'He's an idiot and I'm going to drive him off the track!' But I'm not an actor; I'm a racing driver and I don't see why I should be anything other than myself.

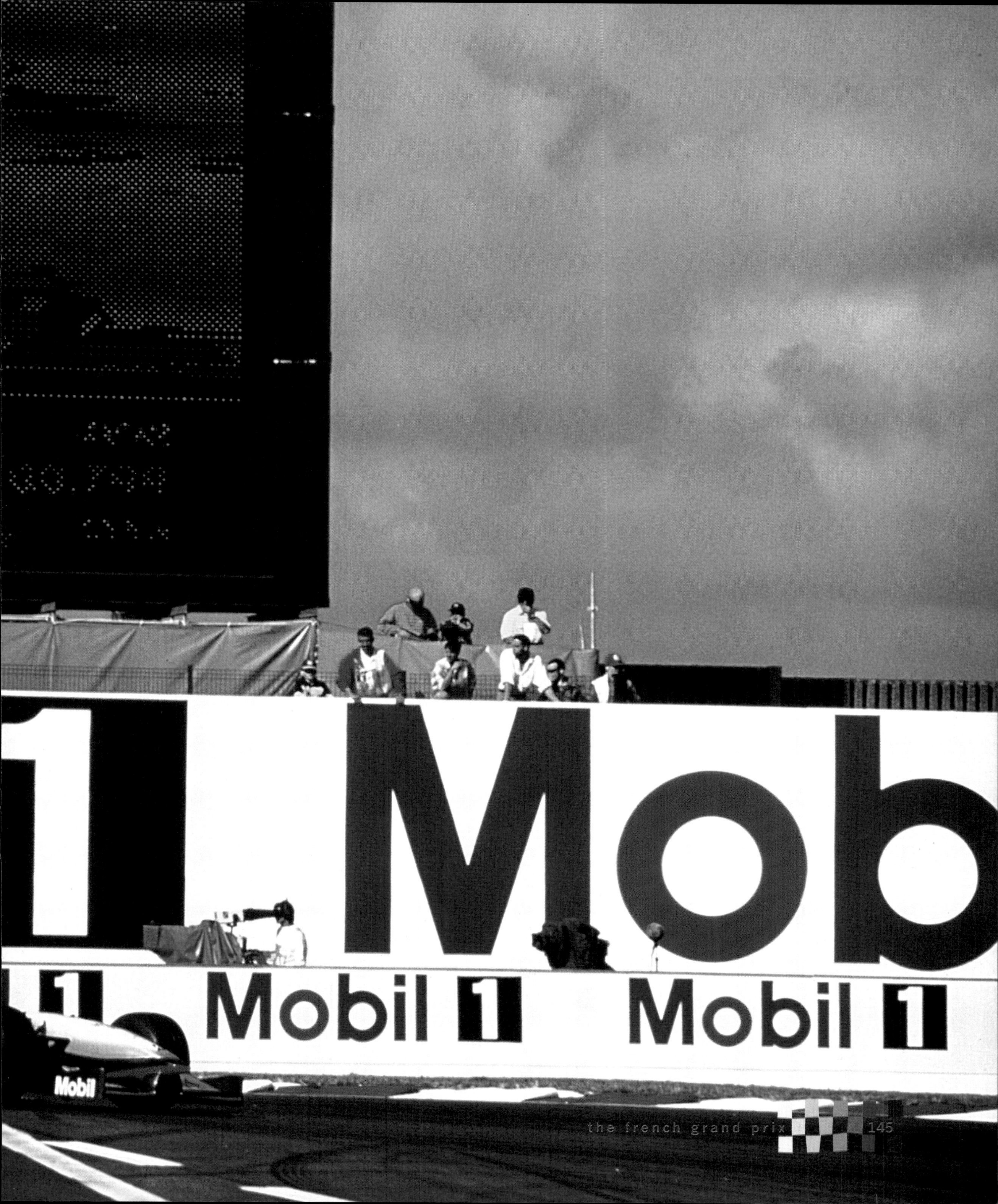
Mob
Mobil 1
Mobil 1
Mobil

© Tap/Hoch Zwei

It's surprising how often you get asked the insulting question: 'How do you feel about the fact that there are no personalities in F1 today?' People ask you that without considering that they are effectively saying: 'How do you feel not having a personality?' It's tempting to say: 'Thank you very much, the interview is over.'

It seems some journalists would prefer drivers who chainsmoke and stay out to all hours in nightclubs, drinking and chasing women, then stagger into their cars on Sunday, drive the hated foreigners off the track and win the race. To some people that might be the definition of personality, but even if there were a few drivers like that in the past there is nobody like that in F1 these days.

A few journalists also try hard to stir up feuds between drivers and teams, and sometimes they are successful. I refuse to co-operate in this kind of thing and that's why I'm never going to be the sensation-seekers' favourite interviewee. The more inflammatory stories you give, the more you are looked upon to do it. I don't see why everything has to be done in public. It just becomes like a tennis match, batting insults back and forth. I'm really not interested in that at all. I just want to do the minimum of media work that's required to satisfy the team and save the maximum effort for what I do in the car.

At the halfway point in the season third in the championship was a position I felt didn't accurately reflect my performances

Even though I'm getting more experienced in dealing with the media I still feel most at home when I'm in the car and left alone. And I still feel very uncomfortable when I'm forced into the public eye when I get out of the car after achieving something worthwhile.

There are no private moments. There is nowhere you can stand in an F1 paddock, either one-on-one or with a small group of people, and expect to be just left there in the fresh air quietly talking. If you want to be left alone to do that, you have to be in a garage or a motor home. You're not locked in, but you are aware of the fact that if you go outside, you've got to get there and back as quickly as possible or else you're going to get caught in a media scrum or some other distraction. Even nipping out to the toilet can take you fifteen or twenty minutes. It's quicker to just pee in a bottle and pour it down the drain! I'm not there for the social side of the sport; I'm there to do a job as a racing driver.

I hope this doesn't sound as if I'm rubbishing my profession. I do recognize that it is pretty marvellous to be well paid to do something that I love and that started as a hobby. I always wanted to compete at the highest level of motorsport, and that is F1. The big motivation is running wheel-to-wheel with another car and trying to figure out what the other driver is thinking and where you can get an advantage. If that great pleasure ever drifts away,

then it would be time to call it quits. It's a great opportunity in life and you've got to make the most of it when you have it because it doesn't last for ever.

Even though I was getting more experienced dealing with the media I still felt most at home in the car and left alone

I love this sport and I'm very protective of it. Anyone who slags off F1 racing is hurting me. I know that it's not wonderful all the time and that the racing isn't always exciting. Nonetheless, the real fans know how F1 works and in the end it is their enthusiasm that is responsible for our sport's existence. I feel very fortunate that a lot of fans follow my career and in the last half of the season I fully intended to reward their support.

Real fans know how F1 works and in the end it is their enthusiasm that is responsible for our sport's existence

As always, my goal was to do my best and finish first, because that's where I think I should be when I do my best. If I won the championship, of course I would be extremely happy. If I didn't . . . well, so be it. But I was determined not to come out of this year of 1998 thinking that I didn't have enough time to work with the team, or I wasn't focused enough to do the job, or that I didn't give it absolutely everything I had. What I had to do now was kick-start the rest of my season, at the British Grand Prix.

grand prix
silverstone, 12 july
Mobil

Mobil
West
LOCTITE
SAP
BOSS
CAMOZZI
BRIDGESTONE
POTENZA

Silverstone

One of my most vivid memories of Silverstone is not from racing, but as a spectator. In 1990 I was there with Paul Stewart Racing, competing in a supporting race for the Grand Prix. On the Sunday morning I rode out to Stowe corner on a scooter and waited amongst a large crowd of people for the F1 cars to come out for the warm-up. I listened closely as the engines were fired up in the pits and when the first car came howling down Hangar Straight towards us through the early morning mist it sent a shiver down my spine. It was a red Ferrari, with its V12 engine screaming at several thousand revs, and that very special moment is something that will stay with me for ever.

In 1995, in my second F1 race at Silverstone, I had the opportunity to give the British fans something to cheer about, when I took the lead in my Williams. As I passed Jean Alesi's Ferrari I could hear the roar of the crowd above the sound of our engines. Then I got a penalty for speeding in the pitlane and eventually finished third. The year before, in what was then my third race in F1, I had finished fifth. With McLaren, in 1996 and 1997, I was fifth and fourth, so Silverstone has been fairly good for me from the results point of view.

The garden party organised by our sponsor Mobil was one of a whirlwind of social engagements at my home Grand Prix

As a driver, not only for those of us who are British, Silverstone is one of the big three races you want to win. The others are Monza, where I won in 1997, and Monaco, where I have yet to win. For those of us in the cockpits, and for the fans, some of Silverstone's landmarks are the best places in the world to drive and to watch F1 cars in action.

Being in Britain you tend to think in miles per hour, instead of the Continental kilometres, but any way you look at it Silverstone is a fast track. Around Copse at 140 miles per

© Sutton

The garden party organised by our sponsor Mobil was one of a whirlwind of social engagements at my home Grand Prix

hour, accelerating up to 175 through Maggots, negotiating the three big S-bends at Becketts at between 110 and 150, through Chapel and up to 190 miles per hour down Hangar into Stowe, braking to about 50 for Vale, accelerating out of Club for the amazing plunge and turn through Bridge at 150-plus, braking hard on the entry to Priory, twisting on the edge of adhesion through the Luffield complex, sweeping around Woodcote at 150, and down the start/finish straight at 175 . . .

I love the place – all 3.194 miles of it – and wish we could have all sixteen races at Silverstone. To win here would be a dream come true.

Friday 10 July

To win here would bring ten points, as it would anywhere else, but your home race does mean more to you than any other. When I went out on the very first lap of practice it was inspirational to see all the support from so many fans. A lot of flags were being waved, both Union

© Tap/Hoch Zwei

Jacks and Scottish flags, and I could hear the cheering over the roar of the Mercedes engine behind my back. It was an emotional moment that gave me a big lift – a nice twinge in the stomach – and took me back to the time I was standing there in the crowd as a wee lad, watching the F1 cars go by. It was a reminder that I was here not just for myself, or the team, but also for thousands of people.

I could hear the Silverstone crowd cheering over the roar of the engine. That emotional moment gave me a big lift

In practice I managed to put all of Silverstone's challenges together into a neat lap that was the fastest of the day, over a tenth of a second ahead of Mika. It wasn't a perfect day, however, and not only because I was fined 8,000 US dollars for speeding in the pitlane! We had spent all the previous week testing here battling understeer and now I found myself fighting oversteer, especially in the medium-speed corners. So being quickest to start the weekend was a bonus. It wouldn't guarantee anything, but it was a great confidence boost leading into qualifying.

Silverstone, formerly an airfield in the Second World War, is quite a flat circuit and that was how I saw the championship situation. I wasn't going to view it as an uphill struggle, and adopt a negative attitude. I was going to try my hardest to win the British Grand Prix and take it from there.

Saturday 11 July

I have mixed feelings about driving in the wet, though I wouldn't say I dislike it

One of the things you often have to contend with at Silverstone is the British weather and in practice we got it in the form of rain. I have mixed feelings about driving in the wet, though I wouldn't say I dislike it. I prefer driving a well set-up car in dry conditions because in the wet if you make a mistake and get onto the grass you are more likely to crash. It's not that I worry about hurting myself, it's just that you have less control over your destiny in the wet. Technically, it's much more interesting to set up the car for dry conditions, while setting it up for a wet track is more of a lottery.

The problem with a wet track is that you have less control over your destiny

I finished the wet practice half a second slower than Mika. I was still struggling to get the car to my liking and began to think it was going to be difficult to beat my team-mate for pole unless I came up with something special. Instead, I came up flat and my worst nightmare came true.

On my first qualifying run it felt as if the rear end was more stable on the track, which was now dry. But somehow there seemed to be a bit less speed than I had had in the morning. I was really taken aback when this was confirmed by my lap time. Despite being in qualifying trim and running with less fuel I was actually slower than I had been in practice. It felt as if the brakes were on, as if I was up against a brick wall on the straights. When I came into the garage we checked over the engine, looked at the data and wondered if the problem might be the stiff wind that was sweeping over Silverstone.

We struggled on but I just couldn't go any quicker. Mika had no problems, nor did Michael Schumacher or Jacques Villeneuve, and by the end of that frustrating hour I found myself in the sorry position of being fourth on the starting grid for my home Grand Prix. It was the most disappointing qualifying session of my F1 career.

It really hurt. I had tears in my eyes. The emotion was just the biggest disappointment I could ever remember

© Tap/Hoch Zwei

© Sutton

I just couldn't believe how wrong qualifying had gone. It was the biggest disappointment I could ever remember feeling

Right: Fourth on the grid really hurt. But with a good race I could still reward the support of the loyal British fans

feeling. When the session was over I jumped out of the car and went straight back to the motor home and lay down. I just couldn't believe how wrong it had gone. It would have been easier to take if the car had felt undrivable, but it hadn't. It felt as if the car was sluggish on the straights, but it was a shock to see what the timesheets revealed. My best lap was nearly a tenth of a second slower than in my morning practice and the 1.039 seconds that separated me from Mika's pole time was the biggest gap in the three seasons we had been together as team-mates.

This was a situation where having Heidi around really helped. She was excellent. We spent some time alone together in the motor home at Silverstone, and back at our hotel later she brought a bit of humour into the evening and reminded me of what I had to focus on. Focus on the race, focus on things like the weather forecast for tomorrow. If it was wet it would be a different race altogether.

RAC
RAC
RAC

Sunday 12 July

At the start I slotted in behind Mika and Michael. Overtaking the Ferrari a few laps later was very satisfying

In the warm-up the track was wet and I beat Mika for the quickest time. We were using his set-up on my car in the belief that the set-up I had used in qualifying had contributed to my poor performance, though we never did find out exactly what was wrong. Before the race I had a conversation with Ron Dennis and Adrian Newey about how to approach the opening laps from fourth on the grid. Their message was to go for it, especially against Michael, and that's what I did

At this stage there hadn't been much more than a light drizzle and the track was only damp with a few puddles

Mika led from the start, Michael was second, Jacques got away slowly and I slotted into third. We were all on intermediate tyres. The weather forecast was for heavy rain some time during the race but at this stage there hadn't been much more than a light drizzle and the track was only damp with a few puddles.

On the fifth lap I came up behind Michael going into Abbey. The inside of the corner was quite wet, but I went for it anyway, drew alongside his Ferrari and was past by the time we got out of the corner. This was very satisfying: being on the limit without going over it in such treacherous conditions and successfully making an overtaking manoeuvre on a driver with a reputation of being unbeatable on a wet track, and one who does not easily give up his position in any conditions. But I was determined that my upward mobility would not end there. My focus was on first place, and over the following laps I waited behind Mika for any opportunity that might present itself – a mistake, while we were lapping other cars, or in our pit stops.

On lap 21 I made a pit stop and went out again on intermediate tyres. The team's information was that the light

© Tap/Hoch Zwei
FOSTER'S
© Sutton

I was pushing hard in the treacherous conditions – too hard as it turned out. In an instant I was aquaplaning out of control

drizzle that was falling would stop in about fifteen minutes. But two laps later, when Mika came in, it was raining in earnest and he was given wet tyres. It rained harder and harder and became obvious that wet tyres were the only ones capable of handling track conditions that before long became diabolical.

Cars were flying off the track at every corner, even aquaplaning off on the straights. In my determination to stay as close as possible to Mika I was pushing as hard as the conditions would allow, even harder, as it turned out. I was sailing by every backmarker that stood in my way. On lap 37 I caught a glimpse of another car ahead of me in the spray as we were approaching Abbey. I pulled out to overtake it, but my car just wasn't equipped to handle the standing water on the track. The light tread pattern on the tyres could not cope and suddenly what little grip they afforded was gone.

In an instant I was aquaplaning out of control. I remember thinking, 'I am going to hit that car' – it was a Benetton – because I knew it would slow right down for the corner. Out of the corner of my eye I saw it whizz past within inches of my car. I flew off the track. I thought about letting the car run through the gravel to the grass strip on the other side so I could rejoin the race. But it stopped just short of that and buried itself in the gravel trap. That was it. Game over.

© Mercedes Benz/Wilhelm

Heidi helped soften the blow, but making my anger and frustration public was something I regretted later

I sat there for a few minutes. I was consumed with anger, for two reasons. I was really angry with myself for making a stupid mistake and falling off the track in my home race in front of over 100,000 fans. But I would probably not have ended up this way if I had been properly equipped. I was very upset at being disadvantaged by the decision to send me out on intermediate tyres while Mika was given wets. I couldn't understand why the team decided to do two different things with our two cars. I trudged back through the mud and stormed into the paddock. I broke my usual rule by speaking to journalists before I spoke to the team. In the heat of the moment I reacted to my feelings, rather than the facts, and probably said more than I should have.

I tried to be diplomatic in my statements to the press, but failed to hide my frustration. Some British papers took up the theme that there were suspicions about Mika being shown favouritism and I didn't do much to discourage them of that notion.

When I left Silverstone that night my feelings were more subdued. I realized that I had simply been a victim of the changing weather conditions and that the decision to send me out on intermediates was based on the information the team had at the time. It was some consolation to find out that eight other cars spun out of the race. Even on wet tyres Mika had a huge spin and was fortunate to finish second, behind Michael.

© Sutton

Ron accepted my apologies for wrongly criticizing the team and assured me I would continue to have its full support

Monday 13 July

When I read the papers on Monday morning I expected that my boss would not be pleased. I got a message to call Ron, but instead I went to see him in person. I think he was happy that I made the effort to go to Woking and get my bollocking face-to-face, rather than on the phone.

Ron said that it was counter-productive for me to be saying negative things about the team in public

In fact, Ron said he wasn't angry but that it was counter-productive for me to be saying negative things about the team in public. He understood the extreme frustration that made me lash out the way I did but, quite rightly, he pointed out that anything that could be disruptive for our team could be capitalized on by our opposition. He assured me that the team was fully behind me and that Mika and I were always going to get the same equipment. I apologized for criticizing the team about the tyre choice and explained that it happened because I allowed emotion to rule my head and that it wouldn't happen again.

We ended the conversation with Ron indicating that, providing we kept performing at our high level, my future with the team was likely to be secure for next season. This was very reassuring to hear, after what I considered to be one of my worst weekends with the team.

My championship hopes had taken a severe knock at Silverstone, where the results left Mika ahead of Michael by just two points. Mathematically, I was still well in contention, at twenty-six points behind Mika with seven races to go and seventy points available to win. But I just had to accept the fact that to get only one point from the last four races is not the sort of way you are going to challenge for the championship.

© Sutton

After the bitter disappointment of Silverstone my plan was to take the next races one at a time and let the chips fall where they may

Luck was not with me. It was bad luck to experience the mechanical problems I had had for three races in a row, and at Silverstone I was unlucky to be caught out on the track at the wrong time on the wrong tyres. You need an element of luck to carry you to the championship and at the moment it seemed 1998 was not going to be my year.

As far as turning things around were concerned, I wasn't even thinking about it. My plan was to take the races one at a time and let the chips fall where they may. I'm paid a lot of money to play in the best racing cars in the world and I would concentrate on just enjoying that pleasure.

West
7
Mobil

the
austrian
grand prix
spielberg, 26 july
BRIDGESTONE
BRIDGESTONE

Friday 24 July

It was satisfying to be fastest in practice on the Austrian A1-Ring after what had been a busy time following the British Grand Prix. We had a full week of testing at Monza where, on the second day, I had a fairly hefty shunt that took the wind out of my sails a little bit. At first I thought it was a problem with the car, but when we looked at the data it showed that I made a mistake in braking and the car went head on into the barriers. The only damage to me was a slight neck strain but the front end of the car needed major repairs. After the guys repaired it, to their amazement I went out and was quicker than ever. As much as they might marvel at it, as an experienced driver you're accustomed to putting such incidents out of your mind and just getting on with your job. In the end, it wasn't much of a setback because by the end of the week I had set the fastest time in the test.

On the weekend after the test I flew to America for Heidi's brother's wedding, and on the Monday I was playing golf in a Duchess of York charity match in the UK. That evening I went back home to Monaco and spent a couple of days training, then went to Austria, a place where we don't have many sponsor functions. That meant that each night was very relaxing, having dinner and chatting with Heidi's brother and his new bride, who came here with us to spend their honeymoon in the beautiful alpine setting where the Austrian Grand Prix is held.

Golf may have been invented in Scotland but this Scot is better at driving than putting and probably shouldn't give up his day job

West
BRIDGESTONE
BRIDGESTONE

I was comfortably quickest in practice but lost out in the lottery of the wet qualifying session

Saturday 25 July

In morning practice Pat Fry worked out a set-up that made the rear of the car very stable, the way I prefer, and I was able to really attack the A1-Ring's tricky corners. I was comfortably quickest in the session and felt confident about qualifying – until the clouds that covered the mountains dropped their load on the circuit.

I knew a wet qualifying session was always going to be a lottery, though I never expected the luck of the draw would leave me with the worst qualifying position of my F1 career.

My poor performance wasn't all down to chance, because at first I had difficulty getting the intermediate tyres to come in, and then kept locking the rear axle on the entry to the corners. On my last timed run I ran wide on one corner and threw away any chance of improving my best time, which had been set earlier, with fifteen minutes remaining in the session. From that point on the track had been drying progressively and the last cars out on the track at the end of the qualifying hour were the ones that ended up with the quickest times. Giancarlo Fisichella's Benetton was on pole, Jean Alesi's Sauber was second, Mika Hakkinen's McLaren was third and his team-mate would start the Austrian Grand Prix from fourteenth on the grid.

Sunday 26 July

Buried back in the pack at the start, I was attacked from all directions. Please, don't anyone else hit my car!

The situation was almost back to normal in the warm-up. It was sunny and hot, and Mika and I were well ahead of the third place man, Michael Schumacher. My strategy for the race was to make one pit stop, hang in there and pass as many cars as possible until the race was over.

Before the race I took a couple of royal passengers on a tour around the A1-Ring in the Mercedes Safety Car. Princess Anne and her husband seemed to enjoy it, and I pointed out the landmarks, where I was about to have a very busy afternoon.

Headed in my direction was a blue car, all locked up with smoke pouring off its tyres

My race start was perfect, though I was surrounded by unfamiliar cars and buried back there in the pack I thought it all looked a bit fraught and unruly. One car stalled in front of me and I had to pull sharply to the outside to avoid ramming it, a manoeuvre that enabled a couple of cars to get by me. As we went up the hill into the first corner my main focus was to try to keep out of the trouble that seemed to be occurring all around me. In my mirrors I saw two cars crash together and two others taking serious evasive action.

The same attitude of self-preservation prevailed as we headed towards the second corner. I was very aware of the cars around me, leaving plenty of space for anybody who wanted to try any heroics that I was certainly not prepared to attempt at this stage. As I braked for the corner I glanced in the mirror to see what was happening behind me and caught a glimpse of an alarming prospect. Headed in my direction was a blue car, all locked up with smoke pouring off its tyres, so I moved well over to the right to give it room to have its accident alone. Instead, it collected me, clipping my rear wheel as it shot past me and spinning me around. The wayward car then sideswiped another car, sending it into a spin. When the driver of that car tried to recover by doing a doughnut – a 360-degree spin – he gave the front of my car a hefty clout.

As I sat there amidst all this mayhem I was saying:

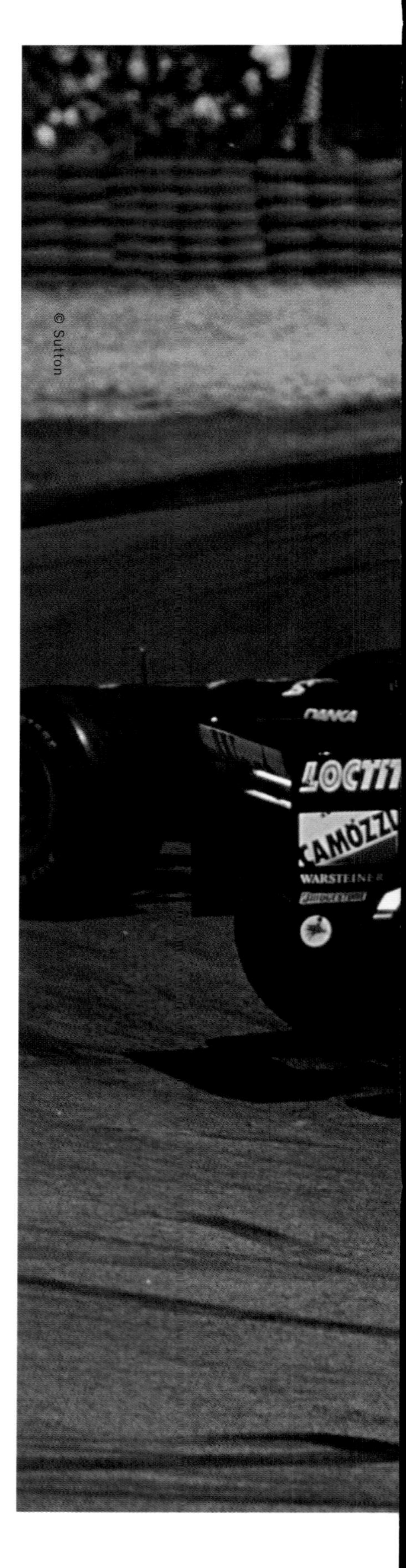

© Sutton

DANKA
BOSS
Mobil 1
Mercedes-Benz
West
West
COMPUTER ASSOCIATES
7
POTENZA
POTENZA
PIAA
YKK
Safra
GOODYEAR

© Tap/Hoch Zwei

© Sutton

After repairs the car was as good as ever and it was very enjoyable picking my way through so much traffic

'Please don't anyone else hit my car!' Maybe they heard me, because all the bumping and grinding stopped. So did the racing, fortunately for me, as the Safety Car came out to give the clean-up crews time to remove several wrecked cars. Mine was still mobile, and as I headed back to the pits I informed the team that the front left of my car had taken a big whack and that there was some damage.

On lap 3, I was in nineteenth place. On lap 28, I was in second place . . .

It took the guys thirty-eight seconds to get me back on track, with fresh tyres and a new nose. Their good work was done while the Safety Car still had the field bunched up and moving slowly. When the signal to go racing again was given I rejoined the track from the pitlane. On lap 3, I was in nineteenth place. On lap 28, I was in second place, behind Mika, and that's the way we finished.

Pat said after the race that overtaking so many cars in such a short time must be some kind of F1 record. Ron said he thought it was an incredible performance and that

© Sutton

From then on it was just a question of keeping the Ferraris behind and stroking it home to finish second

perhaps this was my best ever F1 race. I was quite taken aback by Dave Ryan's comments. I can't remember his exact words, but he rattled off some of the names of the great F1 heroes and for him to put my name up there amongst them was quite special. The compliments were very good to hear, but from my point of view the comeback was fairly straightforward.

Ron said he thought it was an incredible performance and that perhaps this was my best ever F1 race

People might assume that to achieve such a comeback you would have to raise yourself to another level, and get yourself all fired up because you're at the back of the pack and angry about it. Obviously, I was disappointed at getting off to such a disastrous start, but I firmly focused my mind on getting to the finish. I was very calm behind the wheel, at first quietly working away to find out how the car was handling after being hit hard. There seemed to be no problem and as the fuel load went down and the tyres wore a bit the performance picked up. On lap 30, I was able to set the race's fastest lap.

Everything was made easier because I had a good car. If I was in a car capable of only the same speed as the cars I was overtaking, it would be a different story altogether. Most

of the credit should go to my car, but I must say it was very enjoyable, picking my way through so much traffic. It helped that all the drivers I overtook were 100 per cent fair about it, and there were no near misses on a tight circuit where you're overtaking at close quarters.

After I had made the climb through the field I still had to make my scheduled pit stop. It sometimes happens as the fuel comes off and the tyres are coming in on a track like this that you wish you didn't have to stop, because the car is just getting quicker and quicker. The handling became a little more tricky after the stop, although by that time there wasn't the same need to push hard. I was more than content to work away at my lap time. I had one little incident when I ran wide, because I turned in a bit late for the corner and got on the marbles. Rather than fight it, which maybe would risk spinning, I let it go and ran wide because I knew I had the space to come back on the circuit. Other than that, there were no real incidents, and it was just a question of staying ahead of Michael, who was running third, and stroking it home to pick up the six points.

It felt great to be back on the podium. The last time was way back in Spain, five races ago. It was especially satisfying to be able to climb up to that second step after such a bad qualifying session. The guys on the team seemed really happy about it, and the comeback was a tribute to them and the strength of our cars. It was also a timely result considering

Paul Monaghan, Mike Negline and the rest of the guys were very pleased. The comeback was a tribute to them and to the strength of our cars

Overleaf: **It felt great to get soaked with champagne again. The last time was way back in Spain, five races ago**

A1

© Sutton

that contract time was approaching. It was important to remind people what you are capable of and what you are worth.

Heidi and I went back to Monaco that night and had a nice evening out, not necessarily to celebrate, but just because it was a chance to get together socially away from the intensity of a race weekend. We enjoy Indian food, so we took her brother and his wife to one of our favourite restaurants. Jerry Powell came along with us and then we went around to the local pub, met up with some other friends and just generally did the rounds of Monaco.

That would be the last chance to take it easy because the next race was only a week away, in Germany. It's the only time during the season where the races are just a week apart. In fact, we were due to be in Germany on Wednesday. This being the home race for Mercedes we were faced with a hectic schedule of functions that would begin with a major media day at Mercedes headquarters in Stuttgart.

With time in such short supply I set about organizing a private flight out of Nice to give me a few extra hours at home. A couple of years ago I would have taken a commercial flight

© Sutton

and sacrificed some personal time, but now it's too valuable. It's amazing how your life changes and you find yourself in a world where you need to act like a jet-setter, even if you don't feel like one.

The enthusiasm of the Mercedes employees was great to see. Mika and I made a point of thanking them for supplying such good engines

Wednesday 29 July

Our promotional schedule for the day started at ten o'clock in the morning, with a tour of the Mercedes factory at Unterturkheim, near Stuttgart. It was great to see the enthusiasm from the employees and Mika and I made a point of saying thanks for supplying us with such good engines. In the afternoon we took turns taking media people around the Mercedes test track and impressing them with various examples of the company's road cars.

In the evening the guests were invited to go on a boat trip and have dinner at a castle in the countryside. Since this was scheduled to go on until midnight, way past my bedtime, I

© Sutton

made arrangements to have dinner with my old friend David Cawthorne and a few of the cameramen who work on the digital TV coverage of the races. It was really entertaining and funny, a good way to relax and wind down from what had been a fairly exhausting time.

Throughout the day there were interview sessions with journalists, a process that can become tiring when it's repeated many times. I put myself into a kind of cruise control and answered the questions, many of which concerned my championship aspirations.

With six races to go I was now thirty points – three wins – behind Mika. There was no way I was going to give up and I would be trying as hard as ever

I explained that it was now a question of facing the statistical facts. With six races to go I was now thirty points – three wins – behind Mika. There was no way I was going to give up and I would be trying as hard as ever, but I was simply not going to be able to win every race and Mika was not going to stop picking up points. I now had my sights set on second place, ahead of Michael Schumacher, who was twenty-two points in front of me.

Ferrari had announced that Michael would be staying there for several years and he was

The visit to Stuttgart included a boat trip to a castle in the countryside and answering questions about my championship aspirations

being paid a great deal of money to do it. He's a great driver and worth every penny of it, but that doesn't make him invincible. He is especially good in the wet, but at Silverstone, in the type of conditions that suit him, overtaking him was not a problem. I certainly don't come up behind his Ferrari and think I can't pass it. Why should I? He's just another car, another obstacle, you have to clear. Granted, because of his skill and experience it is more difficult to get by him, but it is not impossible, as some believe.

My racing life would continue even if I didn't become the 1998 world champion. I still wanted that title badly and remaining with McLaren would give me the best opportunity, if not now, then next year. I didn't know exactly when the team was going to make it public, but sometime over the weekend of the German Grand Prix I expected it would be announced that Mika and I would be staying with West McLaren Mercedes next year.

© Sutton

the
german
grand prix

hockenheim, 2 august

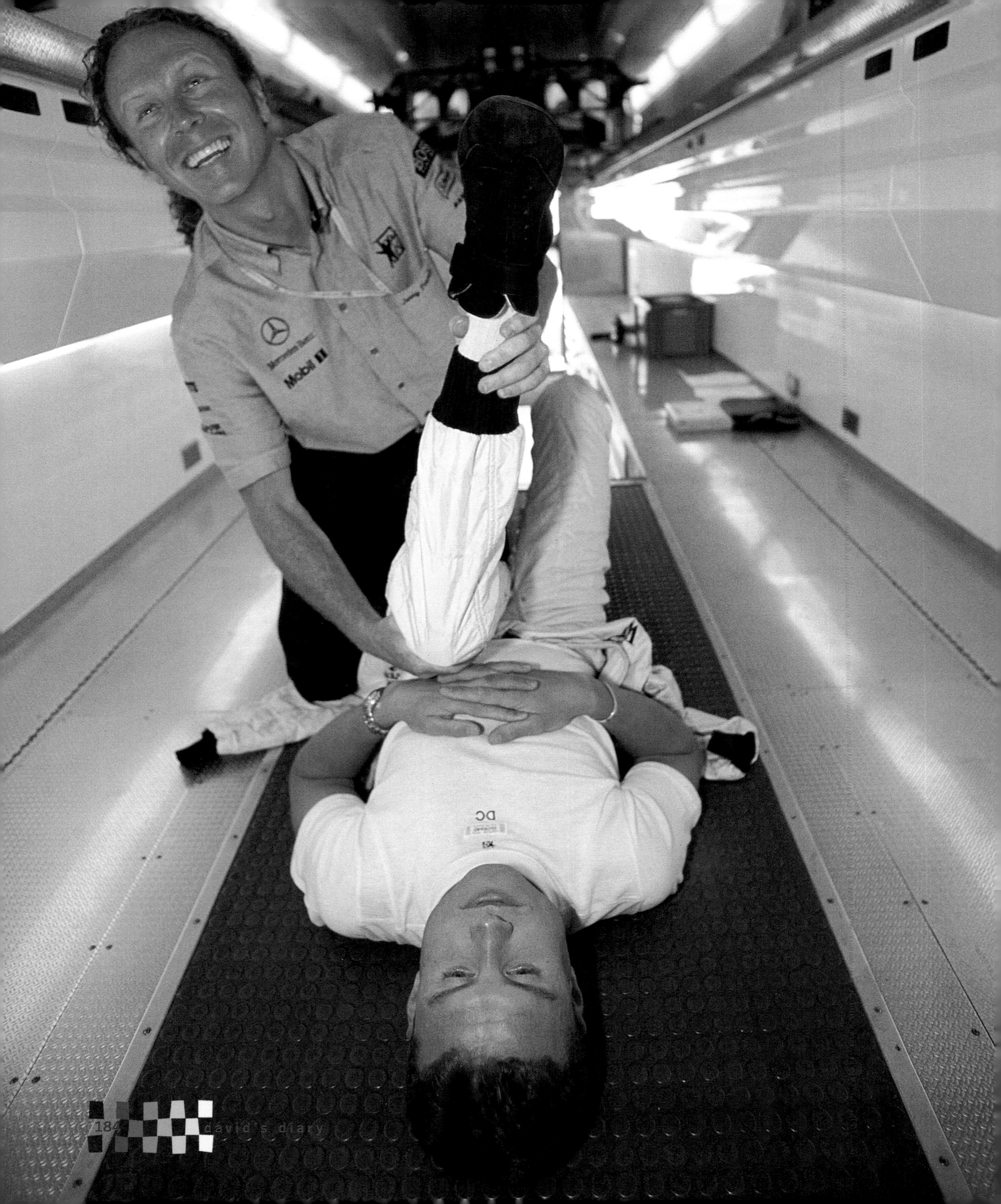
Mobil
DC

Friday 31 July

Mercedes and McLaren's major partner West, which is also headquartered in Germany, had scheduled driver appearances every day over the race weekend, and we also had to perform for our fuel and lubricant supplier Mobil, and our tyre supplier Bridgestone. At these sessions, which took place with their guests in the VIP suites in the paddock, Mika and I appeared in our racing overalls to add a realistic effect. It seemed that every time we got out of the car we were hauled away by our marketing people on one of these special missions. We had to grin and look famous and answer questions about how things were going and what we thought about the Hockenheimring.

I enjoy this circuit, which is a bit like two stretches of autobahn, with some chicanes in the middle of each one, tied together with more kinks and corners at either end. I have raced here since 1990 and in F1 cars the big challenge is to brake from the highest speeds of the season, around 217 miles per hour, to less than 62 miles at a couple of the tighter corners. You have to do this several times on every lap and it does tend to focus the mind. It looks fairly straightforward, but not from behind the wheel, because you make about forty-four gear changes on every lap.

Jerry Powell enjoys putting a suffering body through its paces. It takes a lot of stretching to fit my tall frame into the cockpit

In practice, in the low downforce trim we use at Hockenheim, I got a tow from Mika down one of the straights, pulled out of his slipstream and clocked a top speed of 220 miles per hour, which Norbert Haug of Mercedes said is a record for three-litre F1 cars. Though there is a speedometer on the dashboard I didn't notice the top speed at that point. I was more interested in my lap time, the best of which at the end of the day was just a fraction slower than Mika's.

The only problem I had was having to deal with a lot of oversteer, especially through the twisting Stadium section of the circuit where the low downforce set-up limited the front-end

In practice my top speed was a record 220 miles per hour. Braking to less than 62 mph for the corners can be tricky and spins can occur

grip on the turn-in to the slower corners. Since this section, with a series of corners in quick succession, is the key to a quick lap I was not as optimistic as I might have been about qualifying.

Saturday 1 August

It seemed qualifying would be a shoot-out between the McLarens

Though both Mika and I had spins in practice I managed to beat him for the fastest time. Since we were comfortably quicker than anyone else it seemed qualifying would be a shoot-out between the McLarens. And so it was, except that my ammunition ran out before the session was over.

On my first run I was quickest, a couple of tenths ahead of Mika. We both improved by over a second on our next runs, with Mika nosing slightly ahead. Then, on my third run, I made it easier for him when I had an engine failure and had to park the car out on the track. As I was coasting to a halt I got on the radio and asked the team for the nearest pick-up location, where I could hitch a ride back to the pits. Fortunately, there was one near by, so I hopped into the waiting vehicle and asked the driver to step on it. He did a great job, steering me right through to the paddock in short order, and I ran into the garage where the T-car was waiting. At some races we each have a spare car but when there is only one its primary set-up is alternated between Mika and me from race to race. This weekend it was Mika's, so the guys had changed the seat and pedals to suit me but there wasn't time to do much about the set-up. Without delay I went back out to try to improve my time in what was left of qualifying.

It felt as if the track had more grip now, though it was difficult to be able to adapt to it quickly in a car that wasn't set up quite right for me and also, as it turned out, had a slight brake imbalance. I gave it a go and pushed hard, but it was always going to be a long shot to improve my time in a different car. In the closing moments of the session the

© Sutton

Mobil 1
BOSS
LOCTITE
SIEMENS
BRITISH AEROSPACE
COMPUTER ASSOCIATES
WARSTEINER
sparco
Mercedes-Benz
Mobil 1
BOSS
COMPUTER ASSOCIATES
WARSTEINER
Coulthard
sparco
1999

© Rose/Sutton

© Sutton

track was definitely improving because other people were getting quicker. I wasn't among them and in the end I was relieved that I managed to hold on to second place.

It was a bit disappointing but it felt good to be back on the front row of the grid again, and Mercedes was delighted to have both cars right up there for the start of their home race.

I felt fairly relaxed about the main event because we knew we had a good race car. Reliability would always be an issue on the Hockenheimring because of the length of time the engine spends at higher revs. But I was really feeling quite comfortable about tomorrow, and for the future a lot further down the road.

A few hours after qualifying Jurgen Hubbert, a member of the board of management of Daimler-Benz AG, announced on behalf of the West McLaren Mercedes team the re-signing of its drivers Mika Hakkinen and David Coulthard for the 1999 season.

In my part of the formal announcement I said I was proud to be part of the team for the fourth year running. I respect Mika and whilst I hope to beat him on every occasion, it is good to have such strong competition within the team. I strongly believe that as a driver my best is ahead of me.

I was very happy to stay put, and didn't really want to go anywhere else. I believed what

After we qualified first and second it was officially announced that Mika and I would stay with West McLaren Mercedes next year

the team had to offer me was the best chance to win races, amidst a good atmosphere, with a lot of camaraderie and team spirit that had been built up over the previous seasons. The continuity helps you as a driver, even down to the little things like knowing where all the switches are on the car. Stability makes a difference, especially when the team is on the way up, the way we are.

It was good to have the future settled as soon as possible so I could concentrate on the rest of the season. So far, it hadn't worked out the way I would have liked, but I was bound to make the best of it, and had the security of knowing I would have a fresh chance next year.

We both made good starts, slotted into formation and traded fastest laps as we put some distance between ourselves and the rest

Sunday 2 August

Ralf Schumacher's Jordan was in my mirrors, which was a bit disconcerting

In the warm-up I was fastest by half a second, despite quite a bit of oversteer with the heavier fuel load. The oversteer would improve as time went by and we planned to stop only once during the race.

Mika and I made good starts, slotted into one-two formation and traded fastest laps as we began to put some distance between ourselves and the rest of the field. In the early stages Ralf Schumacher's Jordan was in my mirrors, which was a bit disconcerting until it became apparent he was running with less fuel and was on a two-stop strategy. When he pulled into the pits I knew we were in good shape.

On lap 17 I set the fastest lap of the race, though the car was still oversteering too much for my liking. It was easy to stay close to Mika and we were seldom much more than a second apart. My best opportunity to get past him would be if my pit stop was quicker than his and it was an attempt to do this that caused my most worrying moment of the race.

Mika made his stop on lap 27 and I was due to make mine a lap later. As Mika went in I noticed from the screen on my dashboard that we were running eight tenths of a second slower on that lap than we had been previously. I knew that

Mobil 1 Mobil 1 Mobil 1

SIEMENS
Communications
Mobil 1 Mobil 1 Mobil 1 Mobil 1 Mobil 1 Mobil 1
BRIDGESTONE BRIDGESTONE BRIDGESTONE

© Rose/Sutton

© Sutton

My only worrying moment came after slightly overshooting the pit stop mark. The guys compensated quickly and no time was lost

if I speeded up to my regular lap time before my stop it could make a crucial difference. But on my 'in' lap I got two slower cars in front of me and that made me so frustrated that I tried to make up the lost time by under-braking into our refuelling area and overshot it by a few feet. If you overshoot by too much it completely ruins the stop because the crew have trouble servicing the car. As it was, the guys had to scramble a bit but the time I had lost in the traffic on the way in cancelled out any chance of gaining on Mika.

The guys are pretty good at anticipating where I will stop. Traditionally, if I'm going to do anything I'm going to go long rather than short, so they are always ready for that. This time I had my eyes fixed firmly on Ian Coates, the front jack man, who was backing up as I came in all locked up. But they were all prepared for me being a bit ambitious and it was mainly a question of Forks Morrow getting the refuelling nozzle on, because he and Patch Vale had to move the hose that much more. But they compensated quickly, did their usual great job and in fact my stop was slightly faster than Mika's.

When I returned to the track we were the same distance apart. From then on we raced as equals – in the same cars with similar set-ups, with the same weight because of the fuel load and the same tyres in a similar state of wear. When you've got two such equal cars it

© Sutton

The way we dominated the race might have looked like a Sunday drive around the Hockenheimring to those watching

makes it very difficult to establish any sort of advantage in other areas. This meant that overtaking Mika was going to be very unlikely.

The way we dominated the race might have looked like a Sunday drive around the Hockenheimring to those watching, but believe me when you're doing 217 miles per hour into the braking areas while following another car and losing what little downforce you have it is very difficult in the cockpit. It is one thing to pass a car with inferior performance but to attempt getting past one with exactly the same as yours is a very risky proposition. When that car is being driven by your team-mate there is far too much at stake to go for glory by hooking right underneath his rear wing, locking up the brakes and arriving in the corner all crossed up. It could all so easily end in tears. I didn't need that for my championship and Mika didn't need it for his. In the end we had a good fight, but there wasn't much chance of any change in the running order.

My second set of tyres was performing better than the first and I was more consistent in the second half of the race. I had called for an adjustment of the tyre pressures before my pit stop and that helped. There was still some oversteer, and I wouldn't say I was as comfortable in the car as I was in Austria, but it was good enough to hang in there, and if Mika had a problem I was right there ready to pounce.

In fact, near the end of the race, Mika did have some slight problems, though one of them also caused a problem for me. The team was concerned that his fuel consumption was greater than expected so to be sure he had enough to finish the race they asked him to change the mixture and that took away some of his car's power. This enabled me to get closer, but being in the dirty air behind his car made my car slide around quite a lot. At the same time there was some fluid coming out of the back of Mika's car, so that for the last five or six laps I had trouble actually seeing where I was going.

© Sutton

After our fifth one-two finish it was nice to have Jacques Villeneuve join us on the podium for the first time this season

When we both had to ease up a bit Jacques Villeneuve, who had his Williams flying in this race, was able to close right up. That was an uncomfortable feeling because I know that if my friend Jacques sees half an opportunity, he will go for it. That's not to say he is mad! He's just a very committed racing driver. So when I saw the gap get down to two seconds I knew that if it got to within a second it was likely he would have a go at me. There was so much fluid coming from the back of Mika's car that my mirrors were completely covered. I couldn't see clearly what Jacques was up to and I had to rely on what the team was telling me on the radio, and on what Gavin Beresford was showing me on my pit board each time I went by our pit.

I didn't really keep track of how many laps there were to go in the race because it was quite difficult to take in two bits of information while concentrating on sticking as close as possible to Mika and fending off Jacques' advances. It was a rather nervous time and quite a relief when we completed the forty-fifth lap and were shown the chequered flag.

I felt good about having signed a contract and was pretty comfortable with everything

Our fifth one-two finish of the season made a very happy result for the team. Ferrari did not have a good day, with Michael collecting only fifth-place points. I had gained some ground on him and our team points put us further ahead in the Constructors' Championship. And if points were awarded for engines Mercedes was leading that category handily. It was a perfect home race result for Mercedes, in front of a lot of their employees and top VIPs.

I came away from the weekend in Germany feeling satisfaction at a job well done from a team point of view. There is definitely a real sense of team play in our organization and a real family-type atmosphere. I felt good about having signed a contract to stay in the family and was pretty comfortable with everything.

LOCTITE
BOSS
Mobil 1
West
COMPUTER ASSOCIATES
7

the
hungarian
grand prix
budapest, 16 august
Mobil

Coulthard
BOSS
HUGO BOSS
West
West
Schweppes
Sun
West

Friday 14 August

The twelfth race of the season would be a crucial one for our team, and for our championship rivals, Ferrari. After two successive one-two finishes we were on a roll and we hoped to continue that momentum in Hungary. But we knew that Ferrari, and Michael, could never be discounted. He had a bad weekend in Germany, where he was under enormous pressure because of the expectations of his home fans on a Hockenheim circuit which was probably better suited for our cars.

The Hungaroring is a completely different kind of circuit. Even though it is out in the wide open countryside north of Budapest there is a lot of track, two and a half miles of it, crammed into a small place. This creates a situation similar to Monaco, where there isn't much room to manoeuvre. Like Monaco, the Hungaroring is an enjoyable track to drive on, very satisfying to get right on a quick lap. With fourteen corners linked by short straights and hardly any places to overtake, grid positions are very important. For this race we had decided to use a wider front Bridgestone tyre with a softer rubber compound to improve the grip, especially for qualifying.

Budapest is a lovely city, though there wasn't much time for sightseeing other than the view from the cockpit

Mika and I took turns being quickest in the two practice sessions, with Michael in third place each time on a track that was wet when practice started then dried out. Though it had some oversteer characteristics my car performed well in both wet and dry conditions, so I wasn't worried about how the weather might develop.

Budapest is a lovely city, though as a driver you rarely see much more than the hotel and the route you take to get to the circuit. A couple of years ago I ventured out into the streets and walked around looking at the beautiful local attractions. There seemed to be a lot of them – certainly from the male point of view! This time, I restricted my sightseeing to a nice little restaurant near the hotel, where I had an enjoyable dinner with a group of friends. After that, it was the usual room-service meals for the rest of the weekend.

Saturday 15 August

© Sutton

In the first part of morning practice I spun over a kerb and damaged the undertray of the car. I was looking for the braking limit on one corner and when I went over that limit I chose to let the car spin, rather than risk damaging the front wing. Replacing the undertray cost me about twenty minutes of the second part of the session, but I finished just a fraction of a second behind Mika, who was quickest, and felt in reasonably good shape for qualifying.

© Tap/Hoch Zwei

Heidi and Mika's wife Erja didn't have much to cheer about in Hungary. My spin in practice was the least of our problems

I was looking for the braking limit on one corner and when I went over that limit I chose

Our wider-front Bridgestone tyres were gripping well, and they had to because the sunny and hot conditions brought out the dust and sand that are always a problem on the track surface here. The other problem on the busy Hungaroring was finding room to get a clear run for a quick lap. On my 'out' lap for my first run there was another car in front, so I had to keep slowing down to give myself room. This meant I didn't really get the tyres warmed up to their optimum temperature and the flying lap was compromised.

My second run, on fresh tyres, was trouble-free, and good enough for provisional pole. I still felt there was room for improvement, though it was obviously going to be quite close, as

to let the car spin, rather than risk damaging the front wing

Mika and Michael were also trading quick laps. On my third run, Mika's was the time to beat and for most of the lap I was on course to do that, until I bounced over the kerbs at the last chicane and wiped out my advantage. There was still a chance for one last effort, but my fourth run was ruined by the dreaded traffic.

Time was running out as I prepared to make the last run. I was just a little bit late getting out of the pits, so it was going to be close to make it over the start/finish line before the chequered flag ended qualifying. On the second-last corner, before the start of my run, the team told me there were ten seconds to go. In front of me was a Minardi, so I tried to

© Sutton

For the ninth time this season we had the front row to ourselves. At first, I was able to keep Michael a respectable distance behind

leave a bit of a gap to it. But one of the Jordans was going slow in the middle of the last corner to get a good start to the lap, so the Minardi also had to slow down. I ended up catching the Minardi and having to overtake it by going off line into the dust at the first corner. There was no way you could do a pole lap having to overtake another car, so I just backed off straight away.

It was very disappointing not to get that last run in, because the gap to Mika's pole time was only 0.158 seconds. At least we had the front row to ourselves, for the ninth time this season, and once again Michael was best of the rest.

Providing Mika and I made similar starts, as we had been doing lately, we would probably run one-two into the first corner and be able to control the race. We had planned for either two or three pit stops, depending on how the race unfolded.

Tactics would be important. It's not until you get into the middle of the race that you get an understanding of where you are relative to the opposition. There was every reason to think that we would still be quick in race trim. Michael got fairly close to us in qualifying, but we felt we were in reasonable shape to have a good Hungarian Grand Prix.

Sunday 16 August

Mika and I were quickest in warm-up and we started the race the same way, with Michael behind us. My strategy in the early laps was to just maintain position, not to push Mika too hard while holding off Michael. I had no trouble doing this, driving well within my limits and keeping Michael a respectable distance behind. Providing I didn't make a mistake, there was no way he could get past me on the tight Hungaroring. Everything went according to plan right up until after the first pit stops. Then everything changed.

Michael made his first pit stop on lap 25, I came in a lap later and Mika stopped on lap 28. We resumed racing in the same order as before, with Mika and me comfortably ahead of Michael. When Michael stopped again, on the 43rd lap of the 77-lap race, it became clear that Ferrari had decided on a three-stop strategy. To cover this, we decided to stop earlier than planned, a tactic that would require Mika and me to get in and out as fast as possible to keep our advantage.

Everything went according to plan right up until after the first pit stops. Then everything changed

I had difficulty getting my third set of tyres to work properly. It was incredibly frustrating

On lap 44 I was called in for my second stop and Mika came in two laps later. Our stops were fairly quick but Michael, who took on less fuel in his stop, was able to get the lead on lap 47 and quickly began to open up a gap to Mika, who was experiencing a handling problem.

The problem was costing Mika, and me stuck behind him, about two seconds a lap. At this stage I didn't realize that Mika was in trouble, so I was being cautious not to try making a dive down the inside that could end in us both going off. When Mika finally moved over to let me by, on lap 51, Michael was fourteen seconds further up the road. I thought, now I'll bring the lap time down to at least what I was doing before my pit stop. But I couldn't. I struggled and was about half a second slower than what I could do before. Besides carrying a heavier fuel load I had difficulty getting my third set of tyres to work properly. It was incredibly frustrating.

No matter how hard I pushed it was impossible to make up the lost time

Michael increased his lead. I couldn't push the tyres any harder. There seemed to be a limit to what I could take from the front tyres under braking and from the rear tyres under acceleration. There was no way I could run at the pace that Michael was running at this stage. He was going flat out to build up enough lead to make his third stop. When I hit a bit of traffic, I was forced to go even slower. By the time Michael came out in front of me after his third stop, on fresh tyres and with the same fuel load as me, it was impossible to make up the lost time.

© Sutton

7
COMPUTER

I crossed the finish line in second place, and for a while I was in a kind of shock. For Michael to win after making one more pit stop than anybody else was a remarkable achievement. But I was still unable to come to grips with not being able to match his pace after my second stop, when I had had no trouble staying ahead of him in the first part of the race.

© Tap/Hoch Zwei

I crossed the finish line in second place, and for a while I was in a kind of shock

Later, we mulled over what had gone wrong. When it was decided to cover Michael's strategy and make our stops earlier than planned, the team had to change over the fuel-rig settings, and that lost us a bit of time. Running with the extra fuel we needed to finish the race left me slower than on the first stint and I couldn't run at Michael's pace. It also took a while for the team to understand the full extent of Mika's problem (which turned out to have been caused by a bolt coming off the front anti-roll bar linkage, which made the handling of his car unpredictable). The delay in my getting past Mika enabled Michael to increase the gap, and the damage was done.

By the time the race was over Mika had fallen back to sixth place, a result that reduced his championship lead over Michael to just seven points. In the team standings Ferrari had closed to within twenty-three points of us. This put us all under more pressure. Mika had lost the cushion of knowing he could fail to finish a race and still take the title. Now, with four races remaining, he would have to keep finishing in front of Michael. That would make it more difficult for me, as well.

My goal in the remaining races was still to finish ahead of Michael, who was twenty-two points in front of me, but I would also have to do whatever I could to help my team-mate. I was happy to do that. The sooner Mika tied up the title, the sooner I would be free to try to win some races before the end of the season.

Our visit to Czechoslovakia was more successful. There was never a dull moment in Prague

Wednesday 20 August

After our problems at the Hungaroring it was encouraging to get back on track in a test session at Monza. There, on Ferrari's home circuit, we were consistently quickest and my best lap was over a second faster that Michael's. Meanwhile, Mika was testing at Silverstone and the whole team was deeply committed to avoiding a repeat of what happened in Hungary. We were trying out different aerodynamic packages and also testing Bridgestone tyres, with a view to going back to the narrower fronts at the next race, in Belgium.

On Wednesday we went to Prague, where our sponsor West had arranged an event to bring a sample of F1 to Eastern Europe. Seeing the sights of Prague was one of the

The enthusiastic Czech fans gave us ice hockey gear and puppets of famous F1 drivers

attractions, though all the activities we packed into the day left us little time to explore. To travel to the various functions we were flown in a huge ex-Soviet military helicopter, whose age worried some of the British Aerospace guests who were with us.

In the morning Ron Dennis, Mika and I attended a series of West McLaren Mercedes press conferences at Prague Castle. In the afternoon we went to the nearby Most circuit, where guests were given rides in our MP4-98T two-seater F1 car. That evening there was an extensive programme in Prague's beautiful Wenceslas Square, complete with a kart race, an exhibition of historic Mercedes-Benz cars and live music. We were paraded around in front of a huge crowd, waving at them, signing autographs and so on. There was never a dull moment.

We met a lot of people and exchanged gifts with some of them. Dominic Hasek, the goal-keeper for the Czech national ice-hockey team and a national hero, gave us team sweaters. We gave him miniature helmets, and Mika and I were also given puppets made in our own images. In keeping with our nationalities Mika, who is Finnish, was given a sledge and I got a set of the Czech equivalent of Scottish bagpipes, an instrument that I can't play, though in Prague I managed to squeeze out enough noise to make bystanders cover their ears.

© Rose/Sutton

© Hoch Zwei/Kunkel

BOSS
Schweppes
CAMOZZI

Saturday 22 August

Returning from Prague I spent the next few days at home training, in preparation for the Belgian Grand Prix at Spa. My trainer Jerry Powell and I often ride our twenty four-speed mountain bikes up into the hills behind Monaco. This weekend I went with one of my Monaco neighbours, Mick Doohan, the motorcycle champion, who also does a lot of his training on two wheels. For our climbing Jerry and I tend to use paved B roads, but Mick uses a lot of dirt tracks and pathways.

When Mick took me out the first time on one of his off-road routes his stamina blew my socks off. It was enlightening to see just how fit bike riders are. Obviously, they spend a lot of their time standing on their bikes, so their legs are really strong. I was determined to uphold the honour of F1 drivers and when we went out again I was a lot closer to Mick. He could see the improvement and we had a bit of fun competing in a private hill climb. I was determined to be his equal before the end of the year.

The elegant fashion model, the horse and the racing driver who suggested the bathtub scene. It seemed like a good idea at the time

Fashionmaker

In her career as a model Heidi is photographed in all kinds of situations. One of her recent assignments was to pose for *Tatler* magazine in a fashion spread devoted to clothing worn in country pursuits. They needed a male model to accompany her and I was given the role. I had done this kind of thing a few times before, but it was the first time we had posed together. It was fun and gave me a chance to admire how well Heidi works in front of the camera. I think she looks very beautiful in the pictures, though I'm not sure about the male model.

The photos were taken in a house in London. It was a major production with about fifteen people working behind the scenes and lots of props, including a horse and a bath-tub. In most of the poses I was wearing clothes from Boss, one of our team's sponsors, though in one shot I wore only wellies. The naked racing driver in the bathtub scene was my idea, just one of those silly things that appealed to my sense of humour. It seemed like a good idea at the time

COMPUTE
ASSOCIATE

the belgian grand prix

spa, 30 august

© Tap/Hoch Zwei

West

Friday 28 August

Like most drivers I love the Spa circuit, one of the fastest and most challenging tracks in the world. It's a throwback to the original concept of road racing, with over four miles to the lap on public roads, which are closed off for the Belgian Grand Prix. The track swoops and swerves around like a giant roller coaster, taking you on a ride that is breathtaking and exhilarating. The adrenalin runs higher here than anywhere we race. It's a fabulous place, tremendously satisfying for the drivers and really thrilling for the spectators.

La Source, Eau Rouge (arguably the most exciting and difficult corner in the racing world), Radillon, Les Combes, Malmedy, Rivage, Pouhon, Fagnes, Stavelot, Blanchimont, the Bus Stop – every corner at Spa is famous in motor-racing lore and the track has been the scene of some of the great qualifying and racing battles in F1 history. It is also notorious for wet weather and for big accidents. Unfortunately, this year's event had both and, sad to say, yours truly was deeply involved.

The adrenalin always runs high at Spa, where it often rains. This time they combined to cause trouble. Too much of it came my way

Practice began on a damp track that dried out progressively. In the first hour I was quickest, ahead of Mika, who spun off when he ran over a wet kerb at Stavelot and damaged his car. Behind us was Michael, whose record of several previous wins at Spa made him a leading candidate to be our biggest threat in the race.

In the last hour I had a spin at the La Source hairpin and aborted what would have been my quickest run on new tyres. My little spin was nothing compared to what happened to my friend Jacques Villeneuve, who had a huge accident at Eau Rouge that sent his Williams slamming into a tyre barrier at 180 miles per hour. He was fortunate to be unhurt and, typical of Jacques, he laughed off what was one of the biggest crashes of the year.

Practice ended with Michael's Ferrari quickest, just ahead of Mika and me, while Damon Hill's Jordan was in fourth place. Like Michael, Damon was a previous winner at Spa and with his Jordan on form we knew he could be a threat.

Saturday 29 August

My race would start badly and get worse. Damon Hill would survive to take a well-deserved win on an otherwise black day in Belgium

In morning practice both Mika and I had spins, Mika at La Source and me at the Bus Stop where I went into the chicane while experimenting with the brake balance on the narrower tyres. Again, our little incidents were overshadowed by a huge shunt at Eau Rouge, this time involving Mika Salo's Arrows, which destroyed itself against the

The hour-long battle for grid positions was one of the closest and hardest fought of the season

© Sutton

© Sutton

barriers. Again Mika was able to walk away, with nothing more than a slight concussion. Not long ago an accident of this size could have had a much more serious outcome, and we were all thankful for the safety improvements made in recent years to both F1 cars and the circuits.

At the end of practice Mika and I were first and second on top of the timesheets, ahead of Damon. By the end of qualifying the three of us were still in those positions, though the

hour-long battle for grid positions was one of the closest and hardest fought of the season.

After the first runs, when I was three tenths of a second ahead of Mika, my time put me on provisional pole. I stayed right up there until the final moments of the session, when Mika managed to throw together a lap that was 0.163 seconds faster.

On my last run I gave it everything I had, though I wasn't able to take Eau Rouge without lifting off. For their ego everyone would like to go through here flat out, climbing up

COMPUTER ASSOCIATES
1
1

© Sutton

the steep hill while turning right then left at very high speed. Besides risking the kind of accidents we saw in practice, if you set the car up only for that part of the circuit you screw it up for the following sections. So you have to make a trade-off for a quick qualifying lap.

At this stage, straying over the limit and catching it, I was still enjoying Spa

I tried taking Eau Rouge quicker than the car was capable of and nearly did a 'Jacques'

As it was, I was so desperate to regain pole that I tried taking Eau Rouge quicker than the car was capable of and nearly did a 'Jacques' – though I was lucky enough to catch the slide before disaster struck. Later, Mika said he stole pole from me by taking Eau Rouge without lifting off, but I was able to see from his telemetry that he didn't do it. I knew the truth! The fact was that I lost time at the Bus Stop, the slowest part of the circuit. Until then I was a couple of tenths up on Mika, and I knew it was going to be close.

Coming into the Bus Stop I tried to shorten the line by cutting across the kerbs. This sent the car bouncing too much, throwing it out of shape for the final section, and I ended up losing all the time I had gained. It was disappointing, but that's the kind of chance you have to take in qualifying because you're always trying to push the limit. As it was, my time left me nearly a second quicker than Damon, who had qualified an excellent third, ahead of Michael.

I agreed with the others that it had been a fantastic session on an amazing track. It's wonderful when your car is working well here, and mine certainly was. You're playing with your entry speed into the corners, to make sure you can get more out of the apex. Sometimes you get it right, sometimes you overcook it. It's all a bit of an adventure. At some tracks, like Monaco, you're pleased when it's all over. But at Spa you wish qualifying would go on and on.

Because Heidi wasn't with me this weekend, and there were no functions or appearances to make in the evening, there wasn't the same motivation to rush back to the hotel.

In the atrocious conditions there was a danger we would lose a lot of cars early on

I dallied around at the circuit longer than I usually do, and spent a pleasant few hours talking to the guys on the team and wandering around looking at Spa's attractions. Martin Brundle and I chatted together for nearly two hours, talking over a few business matters and about life in general. It was all very enjoyable and I went to bed that night feeling relaxed and looking forward to the challenges of the next day. In my wildest dreams I couldn't have imagined just how difficult those challenges would be.

Sunday 30 August

As it turned out, a few seconds after the start my worst fears were realized

In the warm-up the rain began that was to continue to fall throughout the race. Also a forecast of what was to come were the numerous incidents of cars sliding off the soaking wet track. More worrying was the lack of visibility when following other cars. In the spray it was difficult to see even the track, let alone the car in front.

Fastest in the warm-up were the Ferraris of Michael and Eddie Irvine. Mika was fourth and I was seventh. I had a spin at La Source and another off-course excursion on one of the downhill sections that damaged the nose of my car. These were minor personal problems but I felt the Belgian Grand Prix faced a bigger one.

About an hour before the start I went to see the race director Charlie Whiting. I hadn't talked to the other drivers, though I was sure most of them would feel the way I did about racing in these conditions. I explained to Charlie that because of the difficulties with visibility there was a danger that we could lose a lot of cars early on, and that it would be a good idea if we started the race behind the Safety Car, until the traffic helped dry out a racing line on the track. I was surprised that this did not happen and, as it turned out, a few seconds after the start my worst fears were realized.

As I sat there on the grid in the pouring rain my visor was steaming up – the last thing you want moments before

© Sutton

West

© Mazzi/Sutton

you're going to need the clearest possible vision. With one eye on the starting lights I reached down between my legs and got the leather shammy and gave my visor a quick wipe. Despite this unwanted distraction I got away smoothly, though Jacques and Eddie made good starts and were on either side of me as we turned into the first corner, La Source. On the exit of La Source Eddie and I banged wheels slightly as we were putting on the power. No damage was done and we were clear of each other as we started down the hill towards Eau Rouge. Suddenly, my rear wheels spun. The car veered sharp right, smashed into the wall, then shot back across the track directly in front of the oncoming pack.

I still don't know what caused me to spin, though it seems likely I just made a mistake,

lost it and from then on was just a passenger. At first I was convinced that I was hit from behind, but when I watched it later on video I couldn't see anyone close. In fact, no one could see anything except glimpses of cars smashing into each other and wheels and debris flying in all directions through the clouds of spray.

It all happened so quickly. I don't really remember many details, after the first hit against the wall. I saw it coming and got ready for more. In that impact my visor popped open and as the car bounced back I grabbed the chinpiece of my helmet with both hands and held on for dear life. I ducked down as low as possible in the cockpit because I was afraid of another car coming over the top and taking my helmet with it.

My car was one of a dozen to be wrecked in the massive first corner pile-up. It was a miracle nobody was seriously hurt

© Bearne/Sutton

© Sutton

For a while I wasn't sure what track we were at. Gradually, it came

I just prayed that my car wouldn't rebound into the middle of the track. But it did and it was destroyed, as were many others. When the red flag came out there were a dozen cars parked there in what looked like a wrecker's yard. It was one of the biggest ever multiple shunts and a miracle that no one was seriously hurt.

I don't know how many cars hit me. My cockpit was a steaming mess, with cold fire extinguisher fluid spraying onto my legs. My left foot was bruised from bashing around in the footwell, and my head had also taken a knock. Mika Salo came up and asked me if I was OK. My natural reaction was to say yes, though I was actually feeling a bit shell-shocked and wasn't entirely positive that I was OK, or even where I was.

When I got back to the garage the team was getting the T-car ready for the restart, which would take nearly an hour while the track was cleaned up. For a while I wasn't sure what track

back to me that we were at Spa and the Belgian Grand Prix would start all over again

we were at. Gradually, it came back to me that we were at Spa and the Belgian Grand Prix would start all over again. Once I got back into the car I felt fine and just focused on making a good start.

The second start was a signal for the accidents to resume. They went on and on

On the second start Mika and Michael touched going around La Source. Mika spun, was hit by another car and his race ended there and then. Halfway around the first lap Alexander Wurz tried to pass me in his Benetton. We collided and flew off the track. Alex was unable to continue. As I was sliding backwards through a gravel trap I selected first gear, let the car slide through onto the grass on the other side and rejoined the race – in fifteenth and last place.

The day after the race Alex sent me a fax saying he hadn't been able to find me at the track to apologize for running into me. He hoped that the incident wouldn't affect our

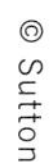
© Sutton

On lap 24 Pat Fry said Michael was coming up behind to lap me and that I should prepare to let him past

personal relationship. I had helped him settle in when he moved to Monaco and we saw each other there occasionally. It was a nice gesture on his part and I phoned him and left a message on his answering machine, saying that I would prefer that he didn't run into me, but there were no hard feelings. There was no animosity after this incident, though there was a lot of it to come.

Cars were flying off the track all around Spa. The Safety Car came out a couple of times while the marshals removed abandoned cars from dangerous positions. But I was making little progress. I wasn't sure whether the rear of my car was damaged in the collision with Alex, so when I came past the pits I slowed down in front of the pit wall so the team could have a look. They couldn't see anything wrong, but I had the uncomfortable feeling that there was some kind of problem, besides having the wrong tyres for the track conditions. It was raining more heavily and I was on intermediate tyres. On lap 9, I stopped to change to full wets and came back out in thirteenth place, second last in what remained of the twenty-two car field.

Meanwhile, Michael was leading the race and the team kept me informed of his

progress. Because of the spray I couldn't see much in my mirrors. On lap 24 Pat Fry said Michael was coming up behind to lap me and that I should prepare to let him past. As I dropped down the hill from Malmedy through Rivage I caught a glimpse of a car approaching, and the marshals began waving blue flags to let me know a faster car was coming up behind me. As I went through the Pouhon corner I maintained my position and my speed on the right-hand side of the track to give Michael plenty of room to overtake me. The next thing I knew there was a massive thump at the rear of my car.

I was shocked! At first, I could not understand what had happened. Then it sunk in. I flicked on the radio and said that Michael had hit me from behind and his Ferrari had just gone past me on three wheels. My car had lost the rear wing in the impact and I came into the pits behind Michael, who somehow managed to make it there on three wheels. The guys directed me into the garage, where I got out of the car. As I was taking off my gloves Michael came running into our garage shouting and screaming at the top of his lungs: 'Were you fucking trying to kill me?!'

I said something like: 'It was you who ran into the back of me, pal.' Michael tried to get

I was shocked. I flicked on the radio and said that Michael had hit me from behind and his Ferrari had just gone past me on three wheels

© Sutton

If he couldn't do it himself he really needed to get some help to control his anger

closer to me, but the guys, led by Roger Duff, held him back. In his fax to me the next day Alex Wurz said that our guys should have let Michael through, because I still had my helmet on. That was the only funny part of this exchange. I was extremely angry at Michael's outburst. I'm afraid I responded in kind and my remarks were widely reported.

I said that for Michael to come into the garage acting like an animal and accusing me of trying to kill him was totally unacceptable and disgusting. If he couldn't do it himself he really needed to get some help to control his anger.

I explained that the team had told me Michael was coming and asked me to let him pass, which I would have done anyway. I was having a terrible race and he was about to lap me, so I was keeping out of his way. Either he wasn't watching in front of him or he couldn't see me in the poor visibility. I hadn't moved over, or swerved, or slowed down. He just drove straight into the back of me.

When I had incidents with him in the past – such as in Argentina earlier in the year, where

he also hit me from behind – I had waited and discussed it with him like a man afterwards. I didn't come stomping down the pit lane asking if he was trying to kill me. I said that until Michael was prepared to discuss it reasonably, man to man, I had no interest in talking to him.

In the heat of the moment Michael accused me of trying to kill him. What I could not accept was his attack on my personal integrity

There were accusations from Michael and Ferrari that I deliberately took him off to help Mika in the championship. I thought this was absolute bollocks – paranoia in the extreme. I said that while it might be understandable in this twisted world that some people would suggest such a thing, you only had to watch the TV footage to see that I was trying to stay out of his way. I expected him to drive around me – not straight into the back of me.

It was completely absurd to think that I would willingly risk becoming involved in an accident that could have been lethal. I had already had more than my share of crashes at Spa and the whole weekend, including the practice accidents, was a wake-up call for us all. In the race the conditions were atrocious, visibility was often nil and there were cars

© Sutton

aquaplaning off all over the place. Before the incident with Michael I had been on the radio for four or five laps, telling them to speak to the stewards and get the Safety Car out for the safety of all the drivers.

With a new wing on the back of my car I went out to finish the race. I was seven laps down, but there was a chance I could collect a point because cars were still dropping out. Just before the finish there was another serious accident caused by the poor visibility. Giancarlo Fisichella's Benetton was destroyed, and briefly caught fire, when it ran full force into the back of Shinji Nakano's slower Minardi.

Only eight cars were still running at the end of a disastrous Grand Prix. I was classified seventh, five laps behind the winner. One of the few positive things to happen in Belgium was Damon Hill's first victory for Eddie Jordan's team. I was delighted for them both and I don't think anyone begrudged them the win in what had otherwise been a black day for the sport.

You can't deny his driving ability and his achievements, but I came away from Spa having lost a great deal of respect for Michael Schumacher

After the race was over the stewards investigating our coming-together called it a racing incident and said that neither Michael nor I was to blame. Though Michael modified his remarks, he refused to change his position that I was responsible for what happened. What bothered me most was the personal attack on my integrity. That is something I place great value on and I could not accept it being questioned.

In our sport we might all have an inflated opinion of ourselves, because you need a lot of confidence to do what we do. But I know right from wrong. I was brought up that way. I did not believe I had done anything wrong; nor did most of those who saw what happened. I could handle Michael being frustrated and angry in the heat of the moment. I could forgive him for coming into the garage and wanting to put his arm around me to have a little chat. But having calmed down, and with the chance to sort it all out in his mind, to not change his position was very disturbing. You can't deny his driving ability and his achievements, but I came away from Spa having lost a great deal of respect for Michael Schumacher.

LOCTITE
BOSS
Mobil 1
West
Mobil

the
italian
grand prix
monza, 13 september

Italy

Following the race in Belgium the incident between Michael and me was now the main story in F1. There had been so much public discussion about it, and so many people had put forward their opinions, that something had to be done to clear the air. For my own satisfaction I felt the two of us should meet to talk through the Spa issue face-to-face. I always believe in taking the direct approach, and that confronting problems head on is the best way to solve them. Even if Michael and I agreed to disagree it would be better than letting the issue simmer away and we could go forward from there.

To help calm things down many people thought it was important that Michael should publicly apologize for his outburst in Belgium before Ferrari's home Grand Prix in Italy. The need to take some kind of action became uncomfortably obvious when we tested at Monza the week before the race. Feelings were running high and when I was quickest in the test it did nothing to improve the mood of the tifosi – the passionate Ferrari fans. Usually, the intensity of their emotions helps create an exciting atmosphere that is inspirational for everyone. But when all that people power is turned against you it can be unsettling.

The passionate Ferrari fans create an exciting atmosphere at Monza. But having all that people power turned against you can be unsettling

Each day of the test there were several thousand fans in the grandstands opposite the pits. While they cheered every move Michael made, especially when he came to the pit wall and stirred them up by waving to them, it seemed about 90 per cent of the tifosi were in an anti-Coulthard frame of mind. I did see one Scottish flag being waved for a while, but it soon disappeared and I wondered if that poor soul was lynched by the angry mob. Most of the rest of them booed and jeered every time they saw me. There were some ridiculous banners saying 'Coulthard Piece Of Shit', 'Coulthard Killer' and so on.

I found this hostility very disturbing. There were fears that some crazy supporter might even attack me. I thought it was outrageous that even though I had done nothing wrong, here

Even Michael's Ferrari team-mate Eddie Irvine thought I was blameless in Belgium

I was in the bizarre situation of being considered a hated villain after an incident that most of the rest of the world regarded as a mistake on Michael's part.

Even his Ferrari team-mate Eddie Irvine thought I was blameless in Belgium. Eddie said there was no way I would deliberately try to put Michael out of the race, because I'm not that type of person. He went further and said that no driver would do that to a colleague. Eddie thought that for Michael to win the race he couldn't afford to lift off, even though he couldn't see where he was going and that he was just unlucky to hit me.

Despite Eddie's beliefs Ferrari issued a press release at the Monza test that didn't exactly calm the uneasy situation. The press release stated: 'Coulthard's sudden slowing down, while on the racing line, was premature and unexpected. Given the poor visibility, the collision was inevitable. Ferrari consider the incident closed. We now look forward to a return to a climate of clean and correct sporting rivalry.'

McLaren responded with a press release stating our team's version of the situation. 'It is our regret that this incident occurred and that its interpretation by Ferrari has challenged the integrity of our team and its driver. It is clear that the incident was accidental and a consequence of the actions of both drivers, who were competing in appalling conditions.'

Some people suggested that Ferrari was using the animosity against me and against the team – based on the absurd inference that McLaren orchestrated my crash with Michael – to put pressure on McLaren to help Ferrari's championship cause in the Italian Grand Prix. Of course, psychological tactics are used in any sport, and if that was the case then at least we knew what we were dealing with. But I was very unhappy about what I felt was the arrogance of Ferrari's position and the unfairness of Michael's interpretation of what had happened in Belgium.

Despite Eddie's beliefs Ferrari issued a press release at the Monza test that didn't exactly calm the uneasy situation

Before we came to the Monza test Michael had admitted publicly that he had over-reacted in the heat of the moment and shouldn't have accused me of trying to kill him. But he still insisted that I had made a mistake. He said he didn't want to believe that I did it deliberately, but he wanted an explanation. So did I – for my own satisfaction and for the good of the sport.

Behind the scenes people on both teams, and others in F1, had tried to arrange a meeting between Michael and me at the Monza test. The idea was that we would thrash out our differences privately and then be photographed shaking hands. It was supposed to happen on Friday, the last day of the test, but Michael didn't show up. I was told that he had to leave early to catch a plane. Later, I was informed that Michael wanted to meet on the Thursday before the Italian Grand Prix and I said I would be happy to do that.

Before and after. For a while, at least, things were looking good for us in Italy. Then Heidi and Erja had to share our disappointment

After the test Heidi and I had a five-day holiday in a lovely villa in Tuscany. Given the hostility of the crowd at Monza I was a bit apprehensive about staying in Italy but we were in a very secluded location and saw few other people. I spent most of the time training around the grounds of the villa, reading, relaxing, and just trying to cleanse my mind and forget all the hassles for a while. This wasn't easy to do because the media, especially in Italy, was playing up the Schumacher-versus-Coulthard 'feud' for all it was worth. The holiday wasn't a very restful period from that point of view, but I felt entirely comfortable with what I knew to be the truth.

Thursday 10 September

When we arrived in the Monza paddock the news that Michael and I were finally going to have our meeting had attracted a lot of attention. There must have been a hundred journalists, photographers and hangers-on gathered around the Williams team's motor home, the neutral territory I had suggested as a meeting place. When I elbowed my way through the crowd Michael was standing on the steps inside the motor home. We said hello and went upstairs. Once we were alone in the room I felt very relaxed, because I had nothing to hide.

We talked about the incident in Spa, how he felt about it and how I felt. We also talked about Argentina again, where our collision took me out of the lead and he went on to win. Michael said I was in the wrong there because I left the door open and then tried to close it on him. In Belgium, he insisted, it was also my fault that we had collided.

I suggested to Michael that he seemed to find it very difficult to acknowledge that he had any responsibility for any incident he was involved in

After offering my interpretation of those incidents I suggested to Michael that he seemed to find it very difficult to acknowledge that he had any responsibility for any incident he was involved in. It seemed he never wanted to admit making a mistake. I told him I didn't think he was taking a balanced view and I didn't think that was correct.

He said I was wrong, that he had apologized to Heinz-Harald Frentzen after taking him out in Canada, and that he had also admitted being in the wrong when he ran into Jacques Villeneuve in the last race of 1997, where Jacques beat him to the championship. I pointed out that Michael had to admit he was in the wrong there because the FIA had found him guilty, and as punishment had taken away all his points scored in the 1997 season.

We went on like this for some time – I'm told our meeting lasted for an hour and twenty minutes – with neither of us changing our positions. At one point I asked Michael if this was the way it was in his private life at home – if he was always in the right and everyone else was wrong. He said that was different. I said it wasn't, that having to strike a balance between right and wrong should be a part of all your life, not just in racing, and that when you are wrong you should admit it.

Michael said a lot of his problems stemmed from the fact that when you are regarded as the best in the sport people become jealous of you. I told him that while I admired and respected his ability I wasn't in the least bit jealous of him – except maybe on the financial side! I added this last bit to lighten things up, but I was very disappointed that he still refused to look me in the eye and admit to any wrongdoing, or at the very least acknowledge that he was not right to question my integrity in Belgium.

However, by the end of our conversation I felt that I had gained, rather than lost anything, because I thought mine was the voice of reason. Near the end of our meeting I said that Michael and I could leave that room in the motor home and never speak to each other again, but that would be a shame because one of the things I most enjoy about being in Formula 1 and performing at the highest level is the fact that you get to interact with drivers from other countries. Michael agreed that that aspect of the sport gave him similar enjoyment and satisfaction. I said that if for no other reason than to prevent spoiling our enjoyment of the sport we should put what had happened behind us and go foward from here. This he agreed to do.

Having to strike a balance between right and wrong should be a part of all your life, not just in racing, and when you are wrong you should admit it

When our meeting was over we were supposed to shake hands in front of all the cameras waiting outside. At first Michael didn't want to do it because he felt it was a political move by McLaren to make him look as though he had backed down from his allegations. I said this was a silly point of view because any reasonable person in Formula 1, surely even on the Ferrari team, wanted an end to a controversy that was doing the sport no good at all. I argued that we should forget about the politics and to prove my point I suggested we could take off our team shirts for the handshake in front of the cameras. He thought about that for a while and eventually agreed to be photographed with our team shirts on.

After our meeting Michael went into a press conference where, though he stopped short of making a direct apology, the things he said made it clear our little chat was not a waste of time. He withdrew the allegations that McLaren orchestrated the crash in Belgium and said it happened because I had chosen the wrong place to let him by, though according to Michael's version of our meeting I had refused to accept the possibility I could have made a mistake.

Any reasonable person in Formula 1, surely even at Ferrari, wanted an end to the controversy that was doing the sport no good at all

Anyway, Michael acknowledged that he did not now believe what happened in Spa was a deliberate act on my part. Michael said that after he had calmed down he realized that I am not the type of person to do this. This was what I wanted to hear, because it was hurtful to have my integrity questioned when deliberately putting another driver at risk is something beyond my comprehension.

Michael said we now had quite a good understanding of each other. I agreed and I looked forward to racing against him again on Sunday – wheel to wheel.

© Mazzi/Sutton

Though differences of opinion remained after our incident in Belgium, Michael and I ended our meeting with a handshake

Friday 11 September

The news that Schumacher and Coulthard had met and had not come to blows put the tifosi in better humour than they had been in the test. There was still some aggression, finger-pointing, shouts of me being a wanker, that kind of thing. And every time our images appeared on the big TV screen in the grandstand opposite the pits the crowd would boo me and cheer for Michael. But it all seemed to be more like a bit of sporting fun, rather than real animosity, and whenever I came face-to-face with a Ferrari fan, regardless of their nationality, I was asked for an autograph. Not one of them said anything unpleasant to me. With Michael and Ferrari so well placed in the championship it was inevitable that the home fans should favour them over us, though we intended to do everything in our power to disappoint the tifosi.

I enjoy the Monza circuit, and not just because I had done well there in the past and won the race in 1997. The combination of high-speed straights and corners, and the heavy braking for the tricky chicanes where you use the kerbs, is challenging and satisfying. We test here quite a lot and I felt pretty confident about doing well.

In practice I was third quickest, behind Eddie and Michael, whose performances gave the

Winning this race in 1997, on a circuit that I enjoy, helped increase my confidence for this year's Italian Grand Prix

The guys did a great job preparing my car. Being quickest in warm-up was good for the morale. The race strategy was simple: go for it!

tifosi something to cheer about. We weren't particularly worried, as we expected the Ferraris to be faster because they were running with much less fuel than we were, no doubt to play to the crowd. I had one high-speed spin through a chicane, when I was really pushing with a touch of oversteer and hit the kerb harder than normal. The car snapped away from me and while it was spinning backwards I was able to turn it away from the barriers and prevent it from stalling. Retrieving the car from that situation helped increase my confidence.

Saturday 12 September

We knew from testing that we had a car that was quick around Monza

Heavy rain in the morning practice, when I was fourth fastest, made the session a wash-out in terms of preparing for qualifying. We had to use wet tyres, there was standing water in many places around the circuit and the visibility in traffic was absolutely terrible.

Fortunately, the weather cleared up, though the track was still damp when qualifying started. In fact, it didn't start until the final twenty minutes of the session, because everybody sat around waiting for the track to dry. With all the action crammed into the last few minutes it was probably exciting to watch, but the traffic jams made our job difficult. Still, I came out of it feeling as if I had hardly broken a sweat, and my time wasn't that impressive either. Grid positions mostly depended on how well you coped with the traffic and I didn't do it as well as Michael, Jacques Villeneuve and Mika.

Fourth on the grid was disappointing, especially when we knew from testing that we had a car that was quick around Monza. But I still felt I was in a strong position for the race.

© Hoch Zwei/Kunkel

West
Coulthard
BOSS
Mobil 1
Mercedes-Benz
West
West
West
BRIDGESTONE

© Hoch Zwei/Kunkel

Sunday 13 September

Being quickest in the warm-up, ahead of Mika and Michael, was good for my morale. So was a race strategy that would enable me to go for the win if the circumstances were right. In the last few races, because of his championship battle with Michael, it was important that Mika should take every opportunity to win. Here, because it seemed I would be quicker than

Mika in the race, and because we weren't on the front row of the grid and Michael was on pole, I should be the one to try to get ahead of Michael. In this way Mika could run a more conservative race to collect points for the driving title, while I could race Michael and, I hoped, get maximum points for the team in the Constructors' Championship.

The two McLarens were in front by the time we got to the first corner. It was the perfect scenario for me

At the start Michael and Jacques didn't react as quickly as Mika and I, and the two McLarens were in front by the time we got to the first corner. Over the next few laps we ran in formation, increasing our lead over Michael, who was in third, and on lap 7 Mika let me

In the lead. I felt there was just no way I was going to lose this race. The Ferrari fans hoped otherwise. Unfortunately, their wish came true

By lap 16 my lead had stretched to ten seconds and I felt there was just no way I was going to lose this race

by. According to our plan, this was the perfect scenario for me, and my equipment felt perfectly suited to getting the job done.

The car was running beautifully and felt so strong. I put my head down and pulled away from Mika at more than half a second a lap. Like everyone else in the race I was on a one-stop strategy and the more the fuel load lightened the quicker I could go. By lap 10 I was over eight seconds ahead of Mika. By lap 16 my lead had stretched to ten seconds and I felt there was just no way I was going to lose this race.

Suddenly, on lap 17, the engine began to tighten and then it blew up. I pulled off the circuit and gave the bad news to the team. I said it calmly, but then added a private comment that I didn't realize the guys heard on the radio. Apparently, they told me later, I've done this before, muttering into the radio before I had the chance to shut it off. What they heard were two words: 'Fuck it!'

It was obviously a major disappointment, to end up sitting there in a cloud of smoke after being on course for what seemed like a sure win. But our troubles weren't over. Because the smokescreen I'd left on the track obscured visibility both Mika and Michael had to slow down, and Michael was able to take the lead. Mika was then hampered by a brake problem and fell back to fourth at the finish. Meanwhile, Michael and Eddie went on to score a one-two for Ferrari and the tifosi went mad.

Before I headed back to the pits I got back on the radio and suggested there might be a risk that after the race my car would be ripped to pieces by the fans. I told the team exactly where it was parked and recommended they send out a couple of heavies to look after it. The car bodyguards arrived and I started walking along the edge of the track, keeping a fence between myself and thousands of Ferrari fanatics. I could have gone into the crowd to try to find a ride back to the pits but even though the fans were mightily pleased to see me walking instead of racing I was still a bit worried about how they would react.

© Sutton

I decided to face the mob. Mostly, they were all smiles, asking for autographs and wanting to shake my hand through the fence

There is no doubt that I was by far the quickest guy at Monza and

I decided to face the mob, waving at them, bowing to them and giving them what I thought was a winning smile. There were a few single-digit signals suggesting I was number one in their hearts. But mostly they were all smiles, asking for autographs and wanting to shake my hand through the fence.

On the long walk around Monza I felt battle weary after yet another failure to finish through no fault of my own. It has happened a lot in my relatively short time in Formula 1. Every driver has a hard-luck story to tell of races they should have won. I don't count races where you inherit the lead and then go out. But when you have led from the start or fought your way to the front a DNF – did not finish – is a hard result to take. All those potential wins are imprinted on my mind. There is no doubt that I was by far the quickest guy at Monza and under normal circumstances I would have won the 1998 Italian Grand Prix. There is some satisfaction in that.

© Sutton

© Sutton

under normal circumstances I would have won the Grand Prix

It was frustrating to be beaten by Ferrari. But whenever we performed to our potential we had won. There were two more races to do it again

The results in Italy left Michael tied with Mika, and Ferrari had moved closer to us in the Constructors' Championship. The standings made grim reading but what was more frustrating was that Ferrari, all things being equal, had never yet beaten us. Apart from Belgium, where they would have won because they were quicker, Ferrari had won races because we had lost them. In every race where we performed to our potential we had won. But Ferrari had made fewer mistakes and had better reliability, and now, with two races remaining, those were two areas we needed to work on.

the luxembourg grand prix

nürburgring, 27 september

Scotland

Between races I managed to squeeze in a rare visit to Scotland, though before that I was gallivanting around Europe. On the Sunday night after the Italian Grand Prix I went back to Monaco for a few hours. The next day I flew to Stuttgart for a promotion organized by our clothing company sponsor Boss, who provided me with some new items for my wardrobe. When it comes to choosing my clothes Heidi, the ultimate shopper, is the boss, so I had strict instructions from her about what garments I should select in Stuttgart.

For the next four days I spent most of the time in my driving suit, testing at the Magny Cours circuit in France. I was doing double duty because Mika was given some time off to help get his head in gear for his championship battle with Michael.

On Friday, I flew back to London to be with Heidi when she won an award at a fashion event. I enjoy watching Heidi on the catwalk, though she never looks at me, sitting there in the front row, gazing up at her adoringly. She says the reason she can't look at me is because if she did she would just start laughing.

Later, we went out to dinner with Jacques Villeneuve and had a very entertaining evening, with lots of laughs, as always. Jacques, famous for his High Grunge wardrobe, was also up for a fashion award, in the most stylish sportsman category, though he didn't win. Maybe he needs a new wardrobe mistress.

Like Jacques, I'm thinking about getting my own motor home and on Saturday I went to look at one. There isn't room in the paddock for drivers to bring a motor home to the races, but since we spend more time testing than racing having somewhere you can call home at test sessions makes a lot of sense. In a hotel, you get what the hotel wants to give you, rather than what you might want. In my own motor home I could have the things I want, like my music.

After a visit to Oxford, to see my business manager Iain Cunningham's new house, we flew to Scotland for some media work and, I hoped, a bit of rest.

Between races I was gallivanting around Europe and managed to squeeze in a rare visit to my native land

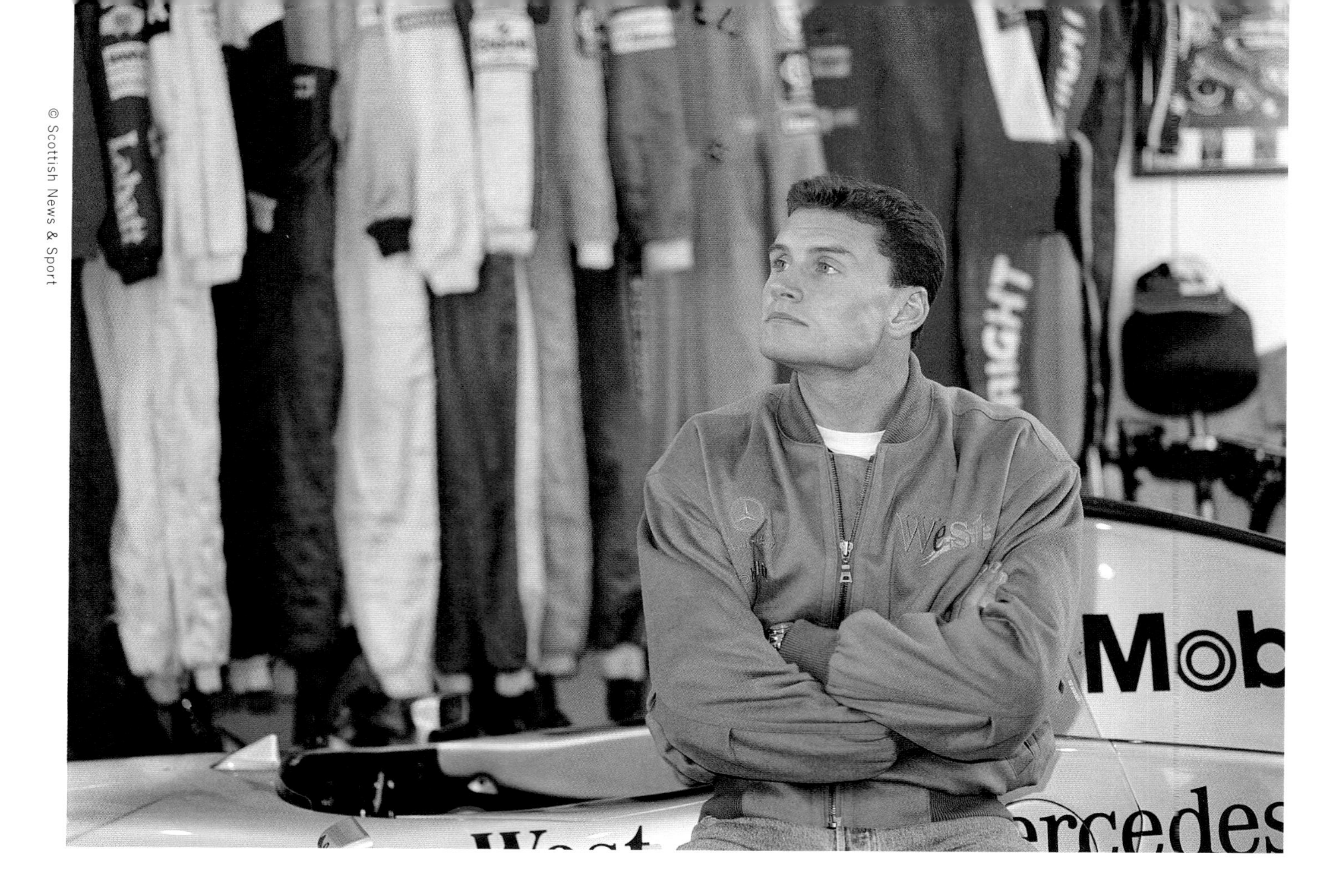

There isn't much time in my life for nostalgia, though the collection of souvenirs in my home village brings back fond memories

On the BBC radio programme *The Morning After* I was asked to select three pieces of music. I chose songs by the Corrs and Queen, and the finale of Giacomo Puccini's opera *Turandot*. Actually, I had to confess on air that it was Iain the opera buff who chose the Puccini piece. He has been trying to get me more interested in opera for some time. I like listening to it well enough but am not really that knowledgeable. Some people think my 1998 season has been like a soap opera. Maybe it could be put to music. The libretto could come from this diary.

I think the Corrs are brilliant, and not just because the girls are beautiful. I'm sure their music will stand the test of time. The piece I chose by Queen was the song 'Who Wants To Live Forever?', which was on the soundtrack of the film *The Highlander*. It was written by Freddie Mercury when he was dying of AIDS. I find it very moving to listen to the lyrics, knowing they were written by someone who knew his days were numbered.

On the last day of my visit to my native land Heidi joined me at the Cameron House hotel on the banks of Loch Lomond. It was beautiful weather, with hardly a ripple on the water, and our time alone in such a peaceful and calm setting was very much appreciated. With our busy careers we don't actually get that much time together in non-stressful situations.

There isn't much time in my life for nostalgia, either, though there is a little building in

Left: **It feels strange now to sit in the Formula Ford that brought me twenty-three wins from twenty-six races when I was eighteen years old**

Above: **Everything s arranged chronologically, from the first overalls I wore as an eleven-year-old kart driver to the latest West McLaren Mercedes outfit**

my home village of Twynholm that brings back a lot of fond racing memories. The David Coulthard Museum is my father's idea. He is the curator and the collector, and started it almost as soon as I began racing karts, when I was eleven years old. At the time I wondered why he even bothered, but now I can see that the cars and memorabilia tell a nice little story and every item there has a special meaning for me.

The collection is not really open to the public but lots of people have heard about it, and usually my proud father shows them around. There is no admission charge but we have a plate where people can make a donation to the Twynholm church. It's not that we're a particularly religious family, but it's a nice little church and to help contribute to its upkeep is a worthy cause.

Among the collection of trophies, photographs, souvenirs, helmets and uniforms are several of my racing machines. My very first kart is there, the one my father bought me as a surprise present for my eleventh birthday. I wasn't too keen to race it, basically because it scared me! But my dad is a lifelong racing fan who grew up watching the likes of Stirling Moss and Juan Manuel Fangio, and he was keen for me to have a go. In my first kart race I was lapped by the leader but won the Best Novice category. And that was it: I was hooked!

My first proper racing car, the Formula Ford 1600 in which I won twenty-three out of

© Sutton

If I want to talk to someone I can blather all day. If I don't, I would rather save my breath for things I enjoy

twenty-six races as an eighteen-year-old in 1989, is still my favourite, though it feels very strange when I sit in it now. In those days we used to drive with our arms sticking out straight, whereas now the steering wheel is tucked right up under your chin. Other winning cars in the collection are the Formula Three I drove for Paul Stewart Racing in 1991 and the Pacific Racing Formula 3000 from 1993, the year before I came into Formula 1.

One of my favourite souvenirs is a framed luncheon menu from the Paddock Club at the 1994 Spanish Grand Prix, where I made my début in the big time. On the menu I have written: 'To Mum and Dad. Thanks for getting me to F1.'

All my racing overalls are arranged in chronological order, from the little blue one I wore in the first kart race right up to the latest West McLaren Mercedes outfit. When people see the collection they remark how neat and well organized it looks, and that is a family trait.

Like my father, I prefer to keep everything neat and tidy. Sometimes I get kidded about being fastidious in the extreme. Even though it may be a bit annoying to others, I believe that if something has to be done you should do it right away, rather than letting it pile up and doing it later. The environment in which I live is very important to me. I can spend more time cleaning up and making things look pretty than I can getting on with serious work.

Thursday 24 September

I thought Mika deserved the championship, because all his race wins had been very clean

The day before the first practice Mika and I had separate press conferences to get the media work over with so that we could concentrate on what was the team's most important race of the season. Both championships were at stake, and with only two races to go, we knew we had to get the best possible results in the Luxembourg Grand Prix.

Naturally, this was the major topic at my press conference, especially the championship battle between Mika and Michael, though I found the constant repetition of the same questions a bit annoying. I sometimes think I'm a weird bugger, and I probably am, but I can't be bothered going through the motions of waffly talk. If I want to talk to someone I can blather all day long, but maybe in my old age I'm getting a bit rude, as I feel that you have a certain predetermined amount of fresh air in your life. If fate dictates how long you have to live, how many heartbeats and how many breaths you will have, I would like to save mine for the things I enjoy, rather than wasting them on what others might want from me. Sometimes during the press conference I felt like just getting up and walking away, but I didn't.

Concerning the team's chances of beating Ferrari, I said we were confident that we still had the best car and it was just a matter of making it work and having the reliability to get the results we needed. When asked if Michael was more likely to win the championship because he is tougher than Mika I said that if the perception of Michael's toughness was based on his many incidents of banging into other drivers, then it was wrong. That was a reflection of his driving style, but in all the incidents he claimed it was the other guy's fault. I didn't call that being tough.

I didn't believe Mika would give an inch because he wanted the championship and if it came down to a wheel-to-wheel battle he would not be found wanting. I thought Mika deserved the championship, because all his race wins had been very clean. Not all Michael's had, including the one in Argentina where he won after hitting me. Given that this is still a sport, I said the best sportsman should win.

In response to questions about Mika being able to handle the pressure, I said that Michael seemed to be making more mistakes this year than in the past. It could mean he is getting older or that he is just driving too close to the edge.

© Sutton

No matter how hard we tried, Pat Fry and I couldn't get rid of the dreaded understeer in my car

Friday 25 September

The Nürburgring circuit is tight, a bit like the A1-Ring in Austria, but with more grip. It has a couple of tricky corners and a few fast ones, and all in all it has a reasonable flow. I was on pole here in 1995 and the next year I got my first podium finish for McLaren. Though the race is called the Luxembourg Grand Prix the Nürburgring is in Germany, making it a home race for our engine supplier Mercedes. In 1997 Mika and I both had engine failures when we were running away with the race, so it was especially important to make up for that embarrassment now.

In practice my car had a load of understeer and I was only able to manage fifth fastest. I was trying hard but the fact that I never actually went off the circuit all weekend highlighted the problem. Normally if I have oversteer, with a nervous rear end on the car, I will go for a run in the gravel at some point because it's quite tricky to balance a car that is nervous. But when you get it balanced I find an oversteering car is quicker. This time, with so much understeer, I never did find the balance you need to have confidence in the corners, which meant a quick lap time was not there.

Saturday 26 September

In morning practice I was able to improve to fourth fastest, but was still struggling with the dreaded understeer. In the wet the car felt better, the best it had been all year. Had the track stayed wet, as it was when we started, I would probably have got a better time. Unfortunately, the Nürburgring was dry again for qualifying.

My best time in qualifying left me fifth on the grid. Besides the understeer, I found some inconsistency from one set of tyres and also encountered traffic that interfered with a quicker lap. Still, it was very close and the first seven cars in qualifying were covered by less than a second.

On reflection I would just have to say Ferrari did a better job than us in qualifying

What was worrying was the presence of the two Ferraris on the front row, with Michael setting the pole time and his team-mate Eddie Irvine getting his best ever grid position. Mika, with similar problems to mine, was third, and Giancarlo Fisichella's Benetton was also ahead of me. Eddie's performance in particular seemed unreal, but that perception was maybe a reflection of my arrogance from being spoiled by having a car that most of the time was capable of getting on the front row. On reflection I would just have to say Ferrari did a better job than us in qualifying.

Sunday 27 September

In the warm-up the situation, from our point of view, was back to normal, with Mika and me setting the fastest times. Still, I wasn't sure if this would translate into our race performance because the opposition might be running with a fuel strategy that was different from our decision to make two stops.

In the warm-up I also made a set-up decision that would affect my race performance, compared to Mika's. While he went in a different direction from what he used in qualifying I attempted to tweak the same set-up I had, in the belief that it would be the best compromise. As it turned out Mika was in better shape for the race than I was.

I made a good start, even better than in Monza, where I qualified fourth and was up to second going into the first corner. Here, I was right behind the Ferraris and ahead of Mika. Under normal circumstances, I might have tried passing Mika on the inside going into the first corner. Instead, because of his championship situation, I let him by and held the inside line, to protect him from anyone diving down the inside and potentially taking him out.

The handling improved throughout the race and near the end I could really attack the track

© Sutton

As it turned out Mika's Ferrari chase was successful and after passing Eddie he was able to catch Michael, then eventually beat him, thanks to an excellent drive, good race strategy and great pit stops. Though I struggled with my handling problem for most of the afternoon, I was still able to help Mika.

In the first part of the race, when I came up behind Eddie he was obviously having his own handling problems, and for some time I was stuck behind him, losing a second and a half a lap over what I was capable of doing. But with my own problem I wasn't able to get out of Eddie's slipstream and try to make a pass. Normally, I would have pitted in this situation but I stayed out longer to allow Mika the best chance to battle Michael. Once Mika had done what he had to do I pitted. The next day Mika called me to thank me for my support, which I thought a nice gesture.

Given my difficulties, I was happy to finish third, and to be able to help Mika, who thanked me for my support

With one race to go, both championships were now within our grasp

Eventually I got past Eddie and had no trouble holding third place, as my car improved after each pit stop. On the first set of tyres I still had to fight understeer. There was more grip with the second set, partly because there was more rubber on the track. On the third set – when I was running with less fuel and had less laps to run to wear down the tyres – the car was much better and I could attack. The fact that I set the second fastest lap of the race just four laps from the finish was an indication of how much I had been struggling before.

Given the difficulties I'd had all weekend I was happy with third place. It was important

to get the car home and get the points we needed for the Constructors' Championship, which was now almost out of Ferrari's reach. Regardless of what might happen in the last race between Mika and Michael, my points total now also confirmed my third place in the drivers' standings, though that didn't leave me feeling especially happy.

My points total now also confirmed my third place in the drivers' standings, though that didn't leave me feeling especially happy

I don't want to sound ungrateful about the opportunities I've had in Formula 1, and I've certainly been very lucky with the cars I've been able to drive, but I've finished third in the championship twice before, in 1995 and 1997. The objective this year was to do better. When my various problems put the 1998 title out of reach, second place became the goal. Obviously, that opportunity had also slipped by. But having to accept the consolation prize again only increased my motivation for the future, and motivation-wise the whole team was feeling sky high after our performance at the Nürburgring.

the japanese grand prix

suzuka, 1 november

West
LOCTITE
SIEMENS
Communications
BRITISH
AEROSPACE
BOSS
West

Preparation

There was a five week interval until the final race of the season but my schedule left me with very little time off. To prepare for the championship-deciding grand finale in Japan we had one of the most intensive testing programmes of the year.

Most of the sessions were at the Barcelona circuit, where I think I must have set a record for F1 testing. Normally, in a full day of testing you do about about 60 laps, but one day I pounded around the track for 160 laps. On other days I ran for 140 and 120 laps. Quantity doesn't always lead to quality but in our case we felt the work we did was very productive and that we were really well-prepared to handle whatever improvements Ferrari might come up with in Japan.

I was very highly motivated to help the team win both championships in the final race of the season

Besides all the mechanical preparation, I made sure the physical side wasn't neglected. Between tests, working with Jerry Powell, I trained harder than ever. When Jerry gave me a fitness test the results showed I was only slightly off the levels recorded before the season started. That was very encouraging, given how inconsistent your training has to be during the racing season.

I was very highly motivated for both testing and training because I wanted to be in top form to be able to make the maximum contribution to the team effort in Japan. Besides wanting to finish this season on a high, for the last few weeks I had been thinking beyond that.

We only needed a single point to beat Ferrari for the Constructors' Championship but the title was theoretically still up for grabs. And Mika's four point advantage over Michael was no guarantee that the Drivers' Championship was a sure thing. Though I felt it would be an injustice if both championships didn't come our way, we still had to win them. As a team player my role was to do everything in my power to make sure that we did. On a personal level, if we achieved both objectives as a team it would help give me a head start on my next objective, which was to become the 1999 champion.

Before the long-haul flight out to Japan I organized my travel gear for the final time this season. Besides the kitbag containing my racewear – several changes of fireproof underwear,

Mercedes-B

Mobil

socks, vests and balaclavas, as well as gloves, boots, helmets and overalls – I always carry a small 'goodies' bag that contains keepsakes from earlier in my career. Nowadays, if I'm given souvenirs I usually give them away to charities but some of the items in my goodies bag have been with me from the beginning.

I wouldn't say I'm superstitious but I have to get into the car from the left side, with the right foot first

There is a St Christopher's medal from my great grandmother, a note my grandmother gave me when I started racing, a gold sovereign from a lady in Twynholm, even a pair of underpants given to me by my Aunt Elaine. They used to be lucky for me and I wore them out many years ago but they still travel with me. Since I've always been a 'just in case' type of person I also bring things like eyedrops, superglue, suntan cream, and so on. Most of the items aren't really practical but it just doesn't feel right to go racing without them.

I wouldn't say I am superstitious, though if I have a choice I will walk around a ladder instead of under it. I also have a ritual for getting into the car. It is strange because it doesn't matter how I get into a road car. But in a racing car, though there is no physical reason for doing it, I have to get in from the left side, with the right foot first. It just doesn't feel right doing it any other way.

Friday 30 October

It was important to get off on the right foot in Suzuka, a circuit where I hadn't done particularly well in the past. Suzuka is right up there with Spa as one of the best in terms of high-speed challenge. I see it as a mix between the Belgian circuit, with long, fast, sweeping corners, and the Hungaroring, with a succession of 'S' curves that flow into one another. The chicane is a bit too tight, but the rest of the track is demanding, physical and very satisfying when you get it right. It's narrow and difficult to overtake and race closely on, but for practice and qualifying it is a great track.

I had a sinking feeling that it was going to be a difficult weekend for me

In practice I was sixth fastest and struggling. From the moment I first hit the track, having put so much effort into preparing for this race, I was very surprised that it didn't feel right. The car seemed to be lacking overall grip and had understeer right from the word go. In the end I was just a couple of tenths slower than Mika, who was fifth, but I had a sinking feeling that it was going to be a difficult weekend for me.

Saturday 31 October

In qualifying I was third on the grid, ahead of Eddie Irvine's Ferrari and Heinz-Harald Frentzen's Williams

While I would do everything I could to help Mika I would stop short of breaking the rules

I picked up the pace in morning practice, though it still felt as if I was playing catch-up in terms of getting a good flow with the circuit and feeling comfortable with the car. Having dialled out most of yesterday's understeer I was able to post a time just a fraction slower than Michael, who was fastest. Mika was third and the most important qualifying session of the year looked promising for the team.

In the end Michael got the best of us in qualifying, taking pole from Mika. My best lap put me third on the grid. I was happy enough with that, considering that I had improved steadily from Friday morning and that I only managed one proper run, the others being spoiled by traffic and then having to slow down when Mika ran slightly off the track in front of me.

The important thing was that I was significantly quicker than the fourth man on the grid: Eddie Irvine in the other Ferrari. In the build up to this race there was a lot of talk about how Eddie and I might help our team-mates in their championship battle. Now, with the four of us on the first two rows of the starting grid, there was the potential for the kind of 'racing incident' that had been a feature of past championship showdowns, a couple of them involving Michael.

While I would do everything I could to help Mika I would stop short of breaking the rules. I had never done that kind of thing for my own championships and I certainly wasn't prepared to do it for someone else's. I would drive as aggressively as usual, and continue to be firm but fair in any close encounter with a Ferrari or any other car.

It remained to be seen exactly how I could help Mika in the race. In a supporting role you have to react to the situation as you find it. From the point in the season when it became obvious it would take a miracle for me to win the championship, I had been effectively covering Mika and protecting him from the others, trying to help him win races

© Sutton

with me coming second, in order to take points off Michael and Ferrari. That is what I would be trying to do at Suzuka on Sunday.

Sunday 1 November

With the rules calling for Michael to take the re-start from the back of the grid his chances of over-hauling Mika for the championship were slim

I was second fastest in the morning warm up and the car felt good in race trim. In fact it felt good throughout the 51 laps of the race. What didn't feel so good was finishing only third in the Japanese Grand Prix, after making a poor start. In fact, there were three starts and it was the last one that I got wrong.

The first start was aborted when a car stalled further back on the grid. The second time around it was aborted again for the same reason. But this time it was the pole-sitting Ferrari that stalled and with the rules calling for Michael to take the re-start from the back of the grid his chances of overhauling Mika for the championship were slim.

Between starts one of our engineers informed me that the telemetry showed my engine rpms were a bit low. To prepare for what finally became the start of the race I concentrated on keeping the revs up and got too much wheel spin. I was also preoccupied with moving across to protect Mika from Eddie, a move that lost me more traction and enabled Heinz-Harald Frentzen to move his Williams past me on the outside.

© Sutton

In the short space of about 100 metres I lost the opportunity to battle with Eddie, who had made it into second behind Mika, and gave myself more work, and frustration, by having Heinz-Harald in front of me. I was probably two seconds a lap quicker than the Williams but had to wait until our pit stops to pass him because I couldn't afford to risk an overtaking manoeuvre. In case anything should happen to Mika's car I needed to be sure of finishing the race for the sake of the Constructors' Championship. The need for us to have this kind of insurance was demonstrated by what happened to Michael's Ferrari.

While Mika was controlling the race from the front Michael was making a big comeback,

The race was started three times. Unfortunately, I got the third one wrong. But in the end it all came right

driving hard, climbing up through the field and into the points. But shortly after the halfway mark his Ferrari ran over some debris on the track, a tyre exploded and he was out of the race and the championship.

With Michael's retirement Mika became the 1998 World Champion. He also went on to win the race. Eddie was second and I had a pretty uneventful race to third. It hadn't been a great weekend for me. There had been too many of those this year. But being on the

Crossing the finish line in front of the best team in the world

podium in the final race gave me some satisfaction and that night I was happy to celebrate both championships with the team.

It was an important occasion: Mika's first championship, the first for McLaren since 1991 and the first for Mercedes in the modern F1 era. One of the first things Mika said to me after the race was that it would be my turn next year, though that may have been partly a way of him thanking me for my help this year. But I was pleased to have contributed to the championships and congratulations were due to everyone in our organization.

I was less pleased about finishing third in the championship behind Mika and Michael, though there was no disgrace in being beaten by people of their calibre. There was also some

consolation in doing as well as I did against two older drivers with more F1 experience. Michael has 117 Grands Prix to his credit and Mika has 112 compared to my 74.

Anyway, I had little time to dwell on what might have been in '98 because I still had work to do at Suzuka. A couple of days after the race I was scheduled to test the Bridgestone tyres we would use next season. After that Heidi and I planned a short holiday in Barbados, and then I would focus on preparing for next year.

A champagne shower for the new champion

West
WARSTEINER

We're number one!
The season-long team effort brought West McLaren Mercedes both the 1998 Drivers' and Constructors' World Championships

postscript

Schweppes
West
KENWOOD
Mobil 1
BOSS HUGO BOSS
West
BOSS HUGO BOSS
WARSTEINER

© Sutton

When I look back over the pages of this diary I feel a mixture of emotions. From the championship point of view there is disappointment because finishing third is something I've done twice before in my F1 career. A goal at the beginning of the season was to improve on that score. My points total in the drivers' standings was higher than in previous seasons but not having won more races is hard to take, considering how good our car was.

The sense of frustration on a personal level is offset by the satisfaction of having contributed to what was a major comeback for West McLaren Mercedes in 1998. As a team we worked better than ever and all our hard work and dedication paid off with two World Championships. It is a great feeling to be part of a winning team and to know that you've been a factor in its success.

As a driver I think this was a year in which I stepped up to a higher level, in terms of working with the team, having a better understanding of race strategy and tactics and making fewer mistakes. In 1998 I made less mistakes than at any time in my F1 career. One thing I learned was that when you can't go any quicker you have to accept it and not do anything silly to throw it all away. Even though you desperately want to win there is no point in going off while chasing after a win that you are never going to get unless the person in front of you goes off. Overall, I think that I matured a great deal as a driver and that next year we will see the fruits of that.

There is an old saying in F1 that to suffer setbacks and have to deal with misfortune is character building. On that basis I must be one of the strongest characters in the sport! I really think that in my 74 Grands Prix to date I've had more mechanical failures while leading races or running in good points-scoring positions than any other driver. It has to be just a coincidence because I don't think it can ever be said that I'm hard on my equipment. Having to deal with this can be terribly disappointing but for the most part I think I handled this year's misfortunes well.

© Hoch Zwei

© Vinet/Sutton

As soon as I was old enough in racing to think I had an opinion that was worthwhile I've always maintained that to be able to compete as a winner you have to be able to handle the failures. Having said that for so many years, since I was a teenager, I think I have convinced myself to accept the failures without letting them get to me in a big way. There were exceptions of course – underperforming in my home race at Silverstone and having the refuelling problems at Magny Cours – where I let the frustrations get the better of me and said things I regretted later. It was just that the stakes were so high and I wanted to win so badly that it became very difficult to accept. On the other hand, I was able to walk away from the setbacks following the mechanical problems that put me out at Monaco, Montreal and Monza, put them behind me, and by the time I got back to the paddock it was as if I'd never been in those races.

It's human nature to try and forget the worst and remember the best, so looking back at the diary entries for the British Grand Prix brings back painful memories. Qualifying at Silverstone was simply awful. Back in the motor home with Heidi I cried because I was so disappointed and upset. Even now it makes me teary-eyed to think about it. I just wanted so much to do well in front of my home fans. That whole weekend, qualifying badly then going off the wet track in the race, was the worst of the year. But the positive thing was that I was quick in the race, passing Michael, pushing Mika and challenging for a victory. There is satisfaction in remembering that, but the bottom line is that when you spin off it's driver error. No matter what caused it – in this case I was on the wrong tyres for the conditions – you're in control of the car and responsible for it.

If Silverstone was the low point of my season, winning the San Marino Grand Prix at Imola so convincingly was a definite high. But the biggest rush of the year for me was in qualifying for Argentina. Getting pole at Imola and Canada were other highlights but Argentina was something special. In the end I was quickest by a considerable margin and I

© Sutton

remember on the slowing down lap I was really whooping it up in the car, making ridiculous noises, cheering to myself – just delighted after putting so much effort into it and getting the result. The rush was similar to a sexual experience. When I describe it that way some people don't think it's a good comparison but I find the feeling of euphoria is very similar.

Compared to my team-mate, who has a reputation for being one of the fastest drivers, I think I performed well. It was very satisfying to outqualify Mika on occasion, to be close to him most of the rest of the time, and to be able to maintain a race pace the equal of his. Because he has the same equipment your team-mate is in one sense your greatest rival. Though that competition helps raise the levels of performance for both drivers you have to be careful that the rivalry doesn't interfere with the team's objectives. In this department Mika and I worked very well together and even though we have completely different personalities we grew into a closer relationship this year.

Mika is an unusual character, very reserved and because of that hard to get to know. But I like him. He's essentially a good person, even-tempered and with no nasty traits. I don't think he would ever deliberately do anyone any harm. Even when we had occasional differences of opinion it was difficult to be angry with him for long. I don't believe he has an argumentative bone in his body. He is just a driver who wants to go racing. People might think it was easy for him to be warmly disposed to me this year because I did all I could to help him win the championship, but I'm sure he will do the same for me next season, when I hope the shoe is on the other foot.

© Hoch Zwei/Kunkel

The team spirit was very high all season and despite all the pressures on us there was surprisingly little friction. Naturally, I was closest to the guys who work on my car and I would like to thank them all for doing a great job. Two people deserve special mention. As the team manager, Dave Ryan has to maintain a balance for everyone but he went out of his way to help me remain confident and feel part of the team. Like Dave, my race engineer Pat Fry is very calm and never bullshits. If I make a mistake he tells me about it quietly. If I do well he doesn't say anything and he doesn't have to. He's just a really straight guy and definitely the best race engineer I've worked with in F1.

Part of the learning experience for me this year was to accept the need to make personal sacrifices for the good of the team. It's not like the karting days or in Formula Ford when you can run your own team, don't have to take orders and don't have authority to contend with. In a big F1 organization like ours you have decisions made for the benefit of the team or the other driver and that is sometimes difficult to accept when you're trying to go all out for wins. But that's the way this sport works and what team play is all about.

Another aspect of this busy season was having even less private time than before. With all the travelling, racing, testing, sponsor appearances and so on, there were long periods when it was difficult to maintain a normal life. From the outside the job of being an F1 driver might look brilliant and some might say they would give up all they have to live the

© Sutton

way we do. I love my job but in some ways I envy those who work a normal number of hours each day, go home at night and have weekends to themselves. This is the way it is for my brother, who works for the family hauling business in Twynholm, has a wife and two children and is as happy as can be. I see that life and I do want to have something like it some day, but it doesn't go with what I'm doing at the moment. It makes it easier that Heidi is often able to travel with me. If she didn't it would be more of a struggle.

Keeping this diary has not been a struggle. I think we all like to talk, especially about ourselves. A lot of it was done in the heat of battle and I only wish those battles had produced more race wins and a championship for me. But maybe a diary with nothing in it but a long string of successes would be boring! I hope this one isn't and at the very least I can say that it is absolutely honest.

David Coulthard
November, 1998

Acknowledgements

Thanks to all my team-mates at West McLaren Mercedes and McLaren International for helping make this such a memorable season to write about and to Ron Dennis for his support of this book.

For their help with photographs I would like to thank Tom Ehman and Pavel Turek at West, Bruce Turner at Mobil, Tricia Greenwood at Marketing Minds and the photographers: Keith and Mark Sutton (friends who have worked with me throughout my career) and Michael Kunkel and Jurgen Tap at Hoch Zwei.

Thanks also to Helen Gummer, Ingrid Connell and Karen Ellison at the publishers Simon & Schuster UK, the book designer Peter Ward, Andrew Benson and *Autosport* for permission to use part of an interview that appeared in that magazine and to Dan Knutson for help with research.

Finally, thanks to Gerry Donaldson (*above left*) for helping me write the book and to Iain Cunningham, whose idea it was.

David Coulthard

November 1998